May the Lord Strengthen
your feet to walk upon
your high places.

Debbie
1405
2022

3 Ways To Enjoying Marital Sex

MARRIED FOR 24 YEARS BUT LIVING SINGLE

The Simple Strategy To Be Delivered From The Mess

Debbie Olabisi

BSc, MBA, Cert CII(MP)

3 Ways To Enjoying Marital Sex

MARRIED
FOR 24 YEARS
BUT LIVING
SINGLE

The Simple Strategy To Be
Delivered From The Mess

Debbie Olukosi
BSc, MBA, Cert CIHMP

ISBN: 978-1-5-136-9213-5

First published in 2022

TABLE OF CONTENTS

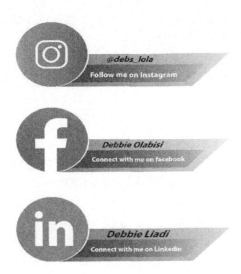

DEBBIE OLABISI

Best-selling Author, A Speaker, Specialist Protection and Mortgage Adviser

This book ranked bestseller in the three categories listed, before its release. And it's been ranking bestseller severally since the past weeks.

See proof below

Product Details

ASIN: B09Q1QKXYZ
Publisher: TriumphInTheMidstofAdversity.Com Ltd (30 April 2022)
Language: English
Text-to-Speech: Enabled
Enhanced typesetting: Not Enabled
X-Ray: Not Enabled
Word Wise: Not Enabled

Amazon.co.uk Sales Rank 5,040 in Kindle Store (See Top 100 in Kindle Store)
24 in Divorce & Separation (Books)
58 in Marriage Relationships
62 in Marriage

About the author

Follow the author to get new release updates and improved recommendations.

Debbie Olabisi

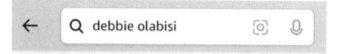

Product Details

ASIN: B09Q1QKXYZ
Publisher: TriumphInTheMidstofAdversity.Com Ltd
(30 April 2022)
Language: English
File size: 4451 KB
Text-to-Speech: Enabled
Screen Reader: Supported
Enhanced typesetting: Enabled
X-Ray: Not Enabled
Word Wise: Not Enabled
Print length: 129 pages

Amazon.co.uk Sales Rank 6,567 in Kindle Store
(See Top 100 in Kindle Store)

26 in Divorce & Separation (Books)

76 in Marriage Relationships

81 in Marriage

About the author

Follow the author to get new release updates
and improved recommendations.

Debbie Olabisi

✓ Following

FOREWORD BY HANNAH KUPOLUYI

Marriage is a lifetime commitment to someone you've chosen as a life partner; and it takes a lot to make it work. A good marriage would mean having a partner with whom you feel liberated sharing your life's emotional highs and lows. However, things become different if you're dissatisfied in your marriage. Finding happiness and fulfilment in daily life when married to someone who you are unhappy with is, simply, tough. And that's what inspired this author in writing this book.

Married for 24 years, Debbie Olabisi felt as though she lived alone. This book shares her first-hand experience, with the main goal of giving the reader a rare, balanced image of the stark realities of marrital life.

It sheds light on her traumatic marriage and reveals things she never knew before taking the leap. Debbie hopes to provide readers a birds eye view of the inner workings of her marital life by leading them through the basic, yet effective tactics she used to get out of the mess and channel her anguish into success.

The book also outlines important, strategic ways to stave off marital storms when they occur, and they will.

Debbie's resilience and fortitude shine through this book without fail, from the first to the last page. I am ecstatic and pleased to write the foreword.

Hannah Kupoluyi

Founder of All Women's Network /
Podcast Host/ Business Coach

Hannah Kupoluyi is a visionary, inspiring leader, and an influencer who has created a platform for women to connect, collaborate, network, and succeed in business and in their personal lives.

She believes that everyone deserves a chance and gives individuals the time, support, and encouragement they need to succeed.

Hannah is a mother of three children. A married, fun-loving, and active woman, she is dedicated to her family and to improving her neighbourhood.

She epitomises hard work and self-discipline with a strong sense of excitement and determination. Hannah has garnered a slew of accolades. As CEO and Founder of "All Women's Network," Hannah's mission is to empower women who want to make a difference in the world by helping them overcome the fears to achieving their goals.

"The Birth Your Vision Coaching Academy," a program that helps female entrepreneurs launch and build their dream enterprises, is her brainchild.

Hannah has supported hundreds of women from dreaming big to achieving their goals. She is a self-made entrepreneur who has hosted Annual Women's Conferences, personal development workshops, monthly networking events, and mentorship sessions to help women gain confidence in starting a home-based business and managing family life.

Hannah is also the host and producer of the award-winning "Birth Your Vision" podcast. Birth Your Vision empowers women in business and aspiring female entrepreneurs by providing inspiration, advice, support, and recommendations on how to expand their business, brand, and visibility. She uses this platform to interview female business guests who share ideas and advice on their journey in business.

ABOUT THE AUTHOR

Debbie Olabisi

Debbie is a practicing member of the Chartered Insurance Institute and the Society of Will Writers. She started her career working in the financial sector and also prides experience in the healthcare and housing sectors. Her passion for helping people birthed Ecarg Financial Solutions and women-supporting charity-Philippians Associates.

At the heart of her core values is doing unto others what she loves for herself. Debbie's day is a success if she puts a smile on your face. Always trying things even if they fail, she is also a go-getter, leaving no room for regrets and never giving up on her goals. **Her mantra? "This too shall pass." Debbie believes intelligent, hard work, focus and strong desire are pertinent for success**.

Debbie holds a first degree in Computer science and a master's in Business administration. She is also a Mortgage & Protection adviser and an estate planner. As a child, Debbie gazed at the night skies and the mysterious stars, hoping she would become an astronaut and be amongst the stars someday. And her life journey epitomizes that - a MIDNIGHT STAR shining in the darkness, lighting up the path for others.

Her days are spent becoming a better self, learning or working. When Debbie is not working, she enjoys reading, listening to music, travelling, taking walks in parks. For up-to-date information about me, connect on social media.

https://www.facebook.com/ecargfinancialsolutions

https://www.linkedin.com/in/debbie-liadi-cert-cii-mp-b427bb27/

Ecarg Financial Solutions (@ecargfinance) • Instagram photos and videos

https://www.instagram.com/debs_lola/

DEDICATION

To God, my Father, my maker, the lifter of my head, my shield in whom I live and move and have my being.... THANK YOU for not allowing your investments in me go to waste.

To My mother- Amoke Olutayo Igbin – whom I never knew, but who loved me so much and sacrificed for me... Burned out before her time like a candle in the wind.

To my adoptive mother - Esther Oyebowale Shonde – you took me in like a daughter and became a mother to me, keeping your word to the letter to a dying woman. Without you, my story is incomplete. I remember my last conversation with you. It was October 2015, when I called you, sobbing. But we could not talk but little because of your environment at the time. And I said mummy please pray for me. I need strength; I can't go on like this anymore. We ended the conversation that morning to discuss later – but alas, the next phone call I received a few days later was news of your demise. You too had gone and left me. I know you are in heaven, praying for me.

I love and miss you both dearly as I daily carry on the baton passed unto me with the assurance of victory. Rest on, my beloved mothers.

To my fathers of blessed memory Alh. Abdul Latif Igbin & Chief Matthew Oladele Shonde – you taught me to be strong, to believe in myself and to never let anyone make me feel or believe less of me. Baba Igbin as we fondly call you, thank you for being there all the way even though I did not get to know you till I was pre-teen, we bonded so much since then. I am indeed blessed to have had you both. I love and miss you both. Rest on in peace

And most of all, To my dearly beloved Children...My Hero and my Shero as I fondly call them. You gave me the reason to keep getting up and keep going ... Without you Sanmi & Princess, I would not have made it this far. Love you both to the moon and back thousand times over. You are the wind beneath my wings.

ACKNOWLEDGEMENTS

I am overly grateful to those who inspired me to write this book, and everyone who accelerated my journey to becoming an author. I am particularly grateful to the editor, proof-reader, book cover designer, Hannah Kupoluyi who wrote the foreword, the reviewers, Abiola Ajibola, Wendy Williams, Olushola, Revd. Emmanuel Oriyomi and all my family and friends who have been instrumental in some way through my journey.

I owe an ocean full of gratitude to many too numerous to mention, amongst whom include:

Kate Iroegbu – A great woman, coach, mentor, friend, sister, and prayer partner, without whom this book would never have come to light.

Tony Morrison – My brother from another mother – who believed in me when I was yet to believe in my strength. Selflessly sacrificed so that I may succeed.

Ebenezer Hundeyin – What can I say - of your wisdom, patience, guidance encouragement and your calmness — when I am raging.

Olabisi Ore – I was lost, like a sheep without shepherd. You found me, soothed me, and helped me get back on my feet.

Olabisi Ajibola – My beloved sis, your wisdom, prayers,

support, can never be repaid – your home has been a safety haven for me.

Esther James – when I was hungry, you fed me, when I was thirsty you gave me water to drink.

Bola Soyoye - In the early days, you always knew when I was losing it and was there to bring me back in form.

Ola Koya - my dearly beloved biggest Aunty.... your selfless love, guidance and encouragement are greatly valued.

Apollos Ikpobe – one time you gave me good counsel, I did not take it and I paid the price, yet you bailed me out. Another time I cried out to you for escape and you said NO, Debbie, you can't go back, you've got to face it- I am grateful I listened.

Pst Bukky OBA – this book would not have been written without you as you connected me to Kate Iroegbu.

Pst Yemi Ajibolorunrin, Pst Thomas Aigbefoh, Rev Emmanuel Oriyomi, Evang Tunde Ayodele-Matthew, Prophet Moses Olurin – My spiritual anchors – I thank God for bringing you into my life and the role you play -- always just a phone calls away no matter what.

God bless you all.

REVIEWS FOR MARRIED FOR 24 YEARS BUT LIVING SINGLE

Review By Mr Olushola Makinwa

**Olushola Makinwa
(MSc, FCCA, FCA)
Krypton Consulting Ltd
(Chartered Certified Accountants & Tax Advisers)
www.kryptonconsulting.co.uk**

I feel honoured to be the first person reading the draft of this book. I met Debbie in 2015, when we both shared the same office building. She came across as a very happy, cheerful, bubbly personality full of life and energy. And it did not take long before we got to know each other, only to find out Debbie came not for friendship but to sell an insurance life cover - I needed none at that time. But I signed on anyways. I saw less of her afterward until much later when her lovely daughter

Princess Aderi'ike came seeking a 2-week placement for mandatory schoolwork experience. Working in the same office building and with an office space to share, I took her in as one of my colleagues for her placement period.

The first few chapters of this book brought me emotional discomfort on one hand, and a sense of elation on the other, because Debbie's journey was so tough she passed through a well: this can be likened to one of the songs of David in the Bible: As she has passed through the valley of weeping, book of Psalm 84: 6 says "When they walk through the Valley of Weeping, it will become a place of refreshing springs. The autumn rains will clothe it with blessings"

The book is a story of love, transformation to hate, triumph over hate and reborn to a full self-attainment. Debbie narrated her tough childhood journey to becoming a loving & caring mother of two children, an entrepreneur determined to succeed in her chosen career and businesses.

This in my view is an example of the teachings in the book of Romans about having strong faith in oneself. Romans 5:3-5.

Suffering builds character. Not only that, but we rejoice in our sufferings, knowing that suffering produces endurance, and endurance produces character, and character produces hope, and hope does not put us to shame, because God's love has been poured into our hearts through the Holy Spirit who has been given to us.

Finally, it can only be hope and faith that held Debbie through her journey so far. This gave her self-belief and strengthened her capacity to endure her way to God-given success. I have no doubt this book is a must-read for everyone, at whatever stage in life. This book demonstrates the power of endurance, hope and faith through our different journeys in life, and I am sure, in her next phase, Debbie will be riding on her successful journey and helping others at various stages of theirs. Many Congratulations Debbie!

REVIEW BY WENDY WILLIAMS

Wendy Williams
Empowerment Coach, Mentor, Storyteller and Public
Speaker; Independent Travel Agent For Bespoke
Experiences

Linkedin.com/in/wendywilliams
Email: wendygbh@hotmail.com

I feel privileged to be reviewing Debbie's first book, written with such depth of thought the writer's feelings and emotions can be felt. Having known Debbie for over 10 years, I know how difficult pouring her soul and thoughts in print would have been. This is stuff you would not want to put down. Pull out tissues out and get ready for an emotional roller coaster.

Your friend and sister always,

Wendy Williams

REVIEW BY ABIOLA AJIBOLA

Abiola Ajibola
Convener - Faith of Eunice. A platform that provides an anchor for children in need. Helping them to overcome barriers to education, facilitating access to education, improving their life chances.

Debbie's story is one of self-discovery. A recap of major life events that left her with more questions than answers. They brought Debbie's vulnerability to the fore, allowing her to push herself through those questions into a realm of re-invention so powerful she became unstoppable!

REVIEW BY REVD. EMMANUEL ORIYOMI

Revd. Emmanuel Oriyomi

The author reveals in this book some of the many mysteries of marital life. What started as honey journeyed her to bitterness. From delicious meals to malnutrition. Fondness to loneliness. Friendship to enmity. From love to hate, and ultimately from happy beginnings to acrimonious divorce. It was everything contrary to God's original plan for marriage - harmony and bonding with true love. Genesis 2:24.

By bringing you closer to a woman who was:

- Married but not loved.
- Married but not cared for.
- Married but lonely.
- Married but abandoned.
- Married but forgotten.
- Married but rejected.
- Married but not 'touched'; and
- Married but Single for 24 years.

The book dives deep into the travails of a rejected wife who eventually turned her misery into triumph through her faith in the Lord Jesus and suggests how people drowned in physical or mental domestic violence could walk out of the mess "in one piece."

Emmanuel Ayinde Oriyomi was born over five decades ago in Victoria Island, Lagos and graduated from Cornerstone Theological seminary, USA. Before surrendering to the will of God in the Christian ministry, I was a teacher, a Hotelier, and a Banker. Reverend Emmanuel Oriyomi is a dynamic gospel teacher, Pastor and a Prophet who teaches about true relationship with God through the person of the blessed Holy Spirit.

INTRODUCTION

The journey as the gold was being refined – an account of my journey so far. I accept myself as I am, wearing my scars physically and emotionally as my badges of honour.

To every person who has ever felt unloved, unwanted, worthless, suicidal, hassled by life, I say to you - NEVER GIVE UP ON YOURSELF.

Because you are one in eight billion - a rare, special individual. There is NO ONE like you and you are here for a good and great purpose. To every person who sees another in dire need – stretch out that helping hand and raise up another fallen hero.

I, who should have been sold for a lamp, have become someone who people rise and turn on a lamp to look at. Ẹnì à bá tá, kí à fi owó ẹ ra àtùpà o tí di ẹni tí aan jí tán ina wo. If it had not been the Lord who was on my side where would I be?

CHAPTER ONE

WHAT IS MARRIAGE?

.

CHAPTER ONE

WHAT IS MARRIAGE?

Many people believe that they want an everlasting marriage, they want their marriage to last a lifetime. Most marriages in the world today end in divorce. While some are not aware of the commitment they are making when entering marriage, many lack the understanding of what it takes to stay married. Although during courtship, intended couples get to know one another and learn from each other's view by talking about important issues like career, finances, religion, the number of children, where to live etc. but things changes as soon as the wedding vows are said. A lot of couples are eager to exchange wedding vows on their wedding day but sadly after that day, they fail to live by the vows. They allow their hectic lives and busy schedule to get the better part of them and they soon start drifting away. They get too busy to spend enough quality time together and this often leads to breakdown in communication which is a vital factor in marriage.

People get married for different reasons, some people get married for wealth, solely to have financial security, some get married because of societal pressure or pressure from their parents, etc. I got married in the quest of a soul mate, someone with whom I can share my life, build a home, and grow old together. A husband that will understand and meet my needs, provide stability (not move from place to place) and direction; that will cherish and delight in me. I wanted a partner that will invest in my life, protect me, and honour me in wise and beneficial ways. But alas, I got the opposite of what I desired in marriage.

God's purpose for marriage

Marriage is the most vital and highest institution in our society. Marriage is God's original plan sketched out. As defined from the beginning, marriage is a blessed union between one man and one woman joined together in unity and indivisibility. After God formed the first man Adam, from dust and set him over the garden of Eden, God soon declared that

> *"it is not good that man should be alone; I will make him a helper fit for him" (Genesis 2:18 ESV).*

God made a woman from Adam whom he caused to fall asleep after which He set in motion an important event that eventually became known as Marriage.

> **Therefore,** *shall a man leave his father and his mother, and shall cleave unto his wife: and they shall be one flesh (Genesis 2:24, KJV).*

Marriage according to the Oxford dictionary is the "formal union of a man and a woman, typically as recognized by law, by which they become husband and wife." It is the state of being a married couple voluntarily joined for life or until the divorce. It is a lifetime commitment which one must make a very important decision before venturing into it. Relationship before marriage and after marriage is quite different, one's aspiration of having a lovely family, being loved, and cared for may not go as expected when one eventually ventures into it.

From experience, the success of a marriage is determined by the choice of both partners. There is no perfect marriage. The secret of a long-lasting and loving relationship in marriage is understanding all the imperfections and differences of both partners as a good marriage is not one-sided, it must be created by both partners.

God designed marriage to bring joy to mankind and glory to Him. Marriage is not part of God's perfect creation; it is God's gift to His perfect creatures. To experience life fully and grow in love for each other in marriage, you must understand God's purpose for marriage.

There are many important concepts in marriage some of which are:

Companionship: True companionship grows out of a oneness of spirit. This occurs in marriage when both the husband and wife can say, "My spouse is my best friend." "Can two walk together, except they agree? (Amos 3:3).

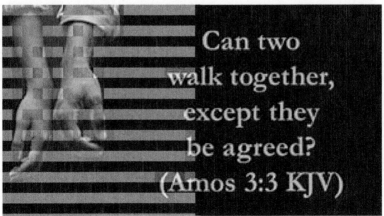

Can two walk together, except they be agreed? (Amos 3:3 KJV)

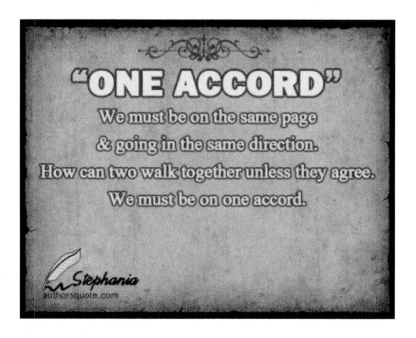

Enjoyment: The principle behind enjoyment is self-control. *"Marriage is honourable [precious] in all, and the bed should be kept undefiled: but whoremongers and adulterers God will judge" (Hebrews 13:4).* God designed Eve to complete that which was lacking in Adam's life. *"And Adam said, she shall be called Woman because she was taken out of Man" (Genesis 2:23).*

Fruitfulness: *"And God blessed them. And God said to them, be fruitful and multiply and fill the earth and subdue it." (Genesis 1:28). "Blessed is the man who fears the Lord, who greatly delights in his commandments! His offspring will be mighty in the land; the generation of the upright will be blessed" (Psalm 112:1-2).*

Protection: The book of Ephesians 5:25 admonishes husbands to love their wives even as Christ loved the church and gave Himself up for her. The husband is therefore expected to protect the wife by laying down his life for her. The wife in return should protect the interests of her home by being self-controlled, hardworking at home, pure, kind, and submissive to her husband to protect the home. (Titus 2:4–5.) Parents are to protect their children to raise Godly children.

Completeness: *"And the rib that the Lord God had taken from the man He made into a woman and brought her to the man. Then the man (Adam) said, "This, at last, is bone of my bones and flesh of my flesh; she shall be called Woman, because she was taken out of Man. Therefore, a man shall leave his father and his mother and hold fast to his wife, and they shall become one flesh" (Genesis 2:22-24).*

Typify Christ and the Church: Humans are to see marriage as a lesson of the divine relationship between Christ and believers. *"Therefore, a man shall leave his father and mother and hold fast to his wife and the two shall become one flesh.*

> *This is a profound mystery that refers to Christ and the church" (Ephesians 5:31-32).*

Things I Never Knew About Marriage

Many people believe that the unmarried are more depressed and unhappy when compared to married ones. I was also of this opinion, but my marriage was an eye-opener. I was born into a Christian-Muslim family. My Christian mother got married to my Muslim father and I was raised by Christian adoptive parents whom I lived with until I got married. My adoptive parents were very affectionate to each other, and they adore themselves so much. They were so close that they practically did everything together. They also understood one another that even we the children never had any inkling if ever when they had any issues. This made me hold them in high esteem and see them as my role models. When I got married to my husband, I imbibed the habit of not letting my anger go to bed with me. I resolved to sort out any issues I had with my spouse or anyone before bedtime.

My family was a peripatetic one. My adoptive father who was a teacher in one of the Unity schools in Nigeria was often transferred from one school to the other. Anytime dad gets his transfer letter, the whole family starts preparing to move with him. In my early childhood I could remember vividly that my travelling expeditions started when dad and mum arrived back from the United Kingdom after their studies. They left us under the care of my paternal grandmother in Abeokuta. I relocated to Janguza, Kano State, Nigeria with my parent when my dad got an appointment as a teacher in the Federal Government College, Kano. No sooner had dad settled down at his new job, than he was transferred to Federal Government College, Ijanikin, Badagry, Lagos and from there he was later transferred to Federal Government College, Minna, Niger State.

I was in my first year in Federal Government Girls College, Bida, Niger State when dad broke the news of his transfer back to Lagos to the family. I love my dad so much; he was my favourite parent. He taught me so much about personal discipline, hard work and dedication. Dad loved me unconditionally. He was in the process of changing my school again, but mum insisted I stayed back in Niger State being a boarding school to continue my education and dad agreed. This decision brought so much relief and happiness to me as it was my first form of stability and will not be losing the few friends I've made. Unlike other times when relocating means losing contact with my friends. The habit of relocating also had some negative impacts in my personality traits. I'm an introvert, very shy, timid, quiet, and well reserved. I grew up a loner and enjoy my own company.

I find so much pleasure in sitting outside alone at night and watching the skies with so many questions running through my mind. Most times I wonder what is up there in the sky, how they got there, what is keeping them there. I would listen to the sounds of the toads croaking and crickets chirping as they rubbed their wings together. I would watch the fireflies as they fluttered about flashing their lights and would sometimes catch them, keep them in a jar for a while and later release them before they die.

The rainy season is my favourite season. I love the pleasant weather with cool breeze and rain shower and most especially the sight of flying termites which is not unusual after the rain. I remembered one of my experiences with termites, it was raining all day and by nightfall, the air was full of winged termites. The annoying insects beat their wings frantically around the tube light outside the house. My siblings and I dipped sheet of papers in oil and tied to the light source. The insects get stuck to the paper, we removed them and roasted them to eat. It's a very tasty snack. I also loved reading. I was a ferocious reader. I would read any book I could lay my hands on. I read everything cover to cover- books, encyclopedias, newspapers, and even the oxford dictionary when I ran out of books to read.

My childhood was full of loneliness and confusion. Sometimes I get very emotional and felt no one understood me. I felt different, different from the others and couldn't understand myself nor have an explanation for what I'm going through. I was very brilliant as a child; I top my class in every term's examination. I was disappointed on one occasion when I came third at the end of an examination. I vowed never to go below the first position and maintained being top of my class till I graduated from secondary school. My dad was always proud of my performance that he would display my results in his office.

One bitter truth I realised when I was a child in my early primary education was that my dad and mum were not my biological parents. It was the end of the term and my teacher handed me my report card, and I thought my surname on the report card was wrong as it was "Igbin", I thought it should be "Shonde". I reported this to my dad, and he confirmed that it should be Igbin. I asked why and, but he denied me an explanation.

That was the beginning of my confusion and endless unanswered silent questions, so Who am I? Who are my real parents? Why am I different? Why did my parents abandon me? Did they not want me? ... and so on....and there began my hunger for love, acceptance, and stability.

Ilé ọkọ ilé ẹ̀kọ́ ni, *ogbo do ni suru* (meaning marital life is a school where you learn to be patient).

These were the words that were sung into my ears during my marriage ceremony. I wondered what they meant and why it was being reiterated. As far as I was concerned, I am a very patient and gentle person. I soon remembered and understood the saying when issues started arising in my marriage.

I was in my fourth year at the university when I got married. I was undergoing my Industrial Training Attachment in Lagos. After the marriage ceremony I stayed at my husband's family home for a couple of weeks (he was living in Oru), I went back to Lagos to continue my industrial training attachment. I had conceived during this period and when my pregnancy advanced my husband deemed it fit for me to stay with his parents.

He secured a position for me in one of the banks in Ijebu -Ode to continue my Industrial attachment. My mother-in-law was a gem, she took care of me, made sure I attended all the modern and traditional antenatal care. I wanted to move back with him to our apartment three months after I gave birth to our son, but he refused and insisted I stayed with his parents till it was time for me to return to school.

The industrial training lasted for eighteen months because the university lecturer also went on strike.

Over time, staying in the family house was like hell for me. I never prepared for all the negative happenings in marriage, neither did I see it coming. Nobody told me I was expected to be a doormat in marriage.

My husband's immediate younger brother embarked on a journey to make my life miserable. It seemed like he had acquired a new servant and being the homely girl I am, I embraced and accommodated my new family with love. I cooked every day for the whole family and will make nice and special meals when hubby is around at weekends. To help me with the chores, I allocate and supervised the cleaning of the whole house to my younger in-laws.

One weekend I did the usual, I allocated the house cleaning chores and my youngest brother-in-law rebelled against helping with house chores. I was surprised at his nonchalant attitude to work and asked him his reasons for not helping with the house chores. He told me that "it was his father's house and that he could do as he pleases". I was shocked and pained by his unruly behaviour and rudeness. After that incident, I stopped supervising the cleaning of the house and maintained my peace by staying in my living quarters. Another thing I never expected in my marriage was being denied of my Christian faith. The family expected me to embrace the Muslim faith. I was raised a Christian and had built a relationship with the Heavenly father.

I was not steadfast in faith when I got married, a lot of challenges had drawn me far away from God. As life situations became more unbearable and threatening, I retraced my steps back to God and cried out to Him. I decided to return to practicing my faith and attended a prayer meeting in church one evening. An emergency family meeting was summoned as soon as my husband got back from work that weekend. My mother-in-law had reported me to him and other members of the extended family. I was still on my knees until the Imam of their mosque walked in and was surprised to see me in that position. My mother-in-law quickly reported my so-called offence to him. She believed he would condemn my action and put the final nail on my coffin. The Imam asked to listen to my side of the story which I narrated. Before getting married to my husband, as a condition, we agreed that I will not practice Islam as a religion nor be buried as a Muslim if I died before him. The Imam asked my husband if there was a mutual agreement between us before marriage for me to practice my faith after I get married to him. My husband reluctantly confirmed he agreed that I practice my faith after marriage. The Imam helped me up to my feet and told everyone I had committed no offence. It was a mutual agreement between us and no one should interfere, I should be allowed to have a mind or will of my own and not be subservient to their wishes and commands. The person they thought would condemn me was the one God used to deliver me.

The Attack (God's Supernatural Saving Grace)

On the day I got married which was just before Christmas, we had two receptions. After the first reception, my dad with misty eyes couldn't hold back his tears as he prayed for me before my husband; and I left for our second all-night reception marriage party at Ijebu Ode. Dad had advised that we leave earlier to avoid travelling late and for security reasons. We did not arrive Ijebu Ode until late in the night all thanks to God. The reception was an all-night party, and the venue was filled with a lot of guests. When it was time for the new couple to join the guests at the reception, I realised the suitcase containing my outfits for the party was missing. As I searched everywhere for it, my father rang to tell me I left a suitcase behind in Lagos and he gave his words to get the suitcase across to me the next day. I was very upset with my sisters for leaving it behind but was relieved it was in safe hands. The best man holding my husband's outfit was also nowhere to be found. My husband and I, had to put on a simple outfit for the reception so there was no way we could be differentiated from our guests, and this made me unhappy that I wore a long face, refused to dance, and went earlier to bed.

At night on Christmas day, (boxing day eve) the whole family were gathered to watch TV, unwrap the wedding gifts and generally have a great time in the living room. After much work, we decided to call it a day and retired to our various bedrooms to sleep. The sound of gunshots woke everyone up, the robbers banged the gate so hard and ordered us to open the door. My father-in-law had fortified the whole house with reinforced burglary proofs that we even teased him that even Kirikiri (a maximum-security prison in Nigeria), was not as secure as what he had done to the house. My father-in-law disconnected the electricity from mains and the whole house was in darkness; everyone went into hiding—kitchen, empty water storage drums, cupboard, wardrobes, pantry, wherever they could find. I laid on the floor in one of the rooms with my mother-in-law shivering.

The robbers struggled with the gate as they tried to gain entry. They fired gunshots which shattered all the glass louvres. For over four hours, they battled with the doors but couldn't gain entry. My brother-in-law and father-in-law got shot and were bleeding. At the rising of dawn, the robbers entered the house through the balcony roof.

One of them switched on the light and a voice who seems to be their leader ordered them to go into the third room and bring out the groom. I was scared, as I wouldn't want them to harm my husband. The robber that was sent to get the groom couldn't locate the room and ended up in one of my brother-in-law's rooms. They soon got all of us out of our hiding places and ordered us into the living room. "Are you not the groom"? the leader of the gang asked my husband who denied saying he was only a guest. The robbers went away with money and valuables. As they were leaving, one of their members was shot by a security guard who was a neighbour.

The robbers dragged their wounded member along but, in a bid, to escape left him behind. As soon as they left, we called out to the neighbours to help drive the victims of gunshots to the nearest hospital because no one in the house could drive.

The robbers were apprehended three days after the bloody attack. One of them confessed that a friend of my brother-in-law conspired with them to rob the couple. I pondered about the whole incident. Are all the bad incidents because the marriage was not meant to be? Have I married the wrong person?

A lot of rhetorical questions ran through my mind, but I was grateful to God for sparing our lives. I was glad after all, that the suitcase containing my outfit was left behind and my husband's best man not showing up with his outfit. It was a blessing in disguise. If we have had our outfits that night, we would have appeared distinguished, danced at the reception, and easily been identified by the robbers. We found out later that the leader of the gang who was instructing his member was also a guest at our wedding reception. Fortunately, he couldn't recognise us because we wore simple outfits and didn't look different from the other guests.

> *"When everything around you seems not to work in your favour if you can pray, reinvent and be open to learning you can turn your situation around"*
>
> *Kate Iroegbu*

For more of Kate's inspirational and motivational quotes get a copy of The Best Motivational Book Ever Written on Amazon.

CHAPTER TWO

THE BELOVED UNLOVED WIFE

CHAPTER TWO

THE BELOVED UNLOVED WIFE

The way he loved me before marriage, was now the reverse in marriage.

Some of our early courtship memories include organized party to mark my 21st birthday, it was fun and everyone in attendance had a swell time. Whenever I spent the night at his place, he would wake me up in the morning to get ready for classes, by the time I came out of the shower he would have selected and ironed my clothes I would wear that day and breakfast would be ready. Our standby cab driver would arrive to take us to the campus. At the close of the day, he would arrive at the agreed time to take us back home. On the days he had to leave before me or days I did not have lectures he would give me assignments to complete before his return and he would check I did them correctly.

In any area I struggled he would take the pain to teach me again until I grasped it. His own mathematics were not your usual 1, 2 ,3 mathematics but rather complex mathematical calculations involving differential equations, dx/dy, double integral sine, cosine, and the likes. For the other subjects like physics or computer programming courses he would make arrangements with his lecturer friends or year 5 students to give me support on topics I found difficult. He made sure I faced my studies squarely... there was no more room for any unseriousness in my academics.

My husband literally worshipped the ground I walked on and for the first time in my life I really felt loved, valued, and appreciated. We were always together, went to the market together, cooked together, shopped together, do the laundry together although he did most of the washing, mine was to rinse and hang out to dry, he would even be with me to get my hair done. He just could barely cope having me out of his sight for longer than necessary. I remember he bought me my first pair of jeans and I refused to wear it and he demanded to know why, I said to him it brought my figure out and I did not want to draw unnecessary attention to myself as I am naturally a shy person. But he insisted, that he just loved to show off his beautiful girlfriend. One time he travelled to Italy for a Mathematics conference he bought me some work suits, one of them was a beautiful brown short skirt suit which when worn to work drew so much attention. Everyone was wowed and my female colleagues where like - you this married woman dressing like this, you don't want to give us single ladies a chance? but when I told them my husband bought it, they didn't believe me. That skirt suit was undeniably a hot number. He has a good taste, himself being a very handsome man and a good dresser.

My wish was his command.... Though I didn't have many wishes as I am a very easy person to please and not at all unreasonable.

Up to this moment, I cannot really explain or understand what made him change and hate me with greater passion than he loved me before. Many nights I've cried myself to sleep, trying to fathom how come he hated me so much, and couldn't bear to be in the same room with me; how much more to touch me.

For you to truly understand, in the later chapters you would see how loving and romantic he was that made me say yes to him.

Loved Like Tamar

Like Tamar, my husband loved me dearly before marriage and hated with great intensity after marriage *2 Samuel 13:1-15*

Here we have the story of the lust-driven affair of Amnon, one of David's sons, and Tamar, one of David's daughters, a half-sister to Amnon. Amnon was sick with love for Tamar, but the fruit of the relationship shows it was not love but lust. He greatly desired to take her to bed, so much so that he deceitfully conspired with his cousin Jonadab to arrange matters. He then compounded that sin by convincing his father for him to be alone with her and raping her The fruit of his shameful deed was further defiled when his feelings for her reversed to hatred that was greater than his former "love." Two years later Amnon was dead at the hand of Absalom, Tamar›s biological brother.

What the piling of sin or coveting produced! It destroyed Tamar's virginity and possibly a future marriage. It destroyed the cohesiveness of David's family. It produced burning hatred, and everyone felt great sorrow. All of this blossomed from an uncontrolled desire in the mind of one person. Its effects impacted on David's family for many generations. He did not love her; he was lusting after her. Notice the initial fruit—distress! The story continues, eventually revealing that his lust produced rape. It did not end there but produced more evil fruit: ***"Then Amnon hated her exceedingly, so that the hatred with which he hated her was greater than the love with which he had loved her. And Amnon said to her, 'Arise, be gone!'" (Verse 15).***

So much for lust producing good fruit! How many teens and/or young adults' lives have been severely damaged by unwed pregnancy resulting from coveting?

Abandoned Like Leah

The Bible is replete with characters from every spectrum of life. We read about great leaders and evil kings.

There are hilarious moments, sorrowful events and amazing connections between God and man. One of such bible characters whose life I often ponder on and resonate with is Leah (Gen 29). She is the elder sister of Rachel and the cousin of Jacob. When Jacob arrives in Haran, at the same well from which his mother Rebekah drew water before she married his father Isaac, he meets Rachel the beautiful shepherdess. Jacob loved Rachael so much but had no wealth to offer as the mohar (customarily given to the father of the bride) so he negotiated to work for Laban her father for seven years as a bride price to marry her.

> Jacob was in love with Rachel and said, *"I'll work for you seven years in return for your younger daughter Rachel, NIV (Genesis 29:18)*

After the seven years of working for Laban was over, the arrangement was not as agreed. When the time to consummate the marriage came on the wedding night, his father-in-law, Laban sent Leah to his tent instead of Rachael. The next morning, in the light of day and the absence of a veil, he received the shock of his life. He was given Leah instead of Rachel.

Jacob protested and Laban told him he could have Rachel after working for another seven years to which he agreed.

[27] Finish this daughter's bridal week; then we will give you the younger one also, in return for another seven years of work."

^{28} And Jacob did so. He finished the week with Leah, and then Laban gave him his daughter Rachel to be his wife. ^{29} Laban gave his servant Bilhah to his daughter Rachel as her attendant. ^{30} Jacob made love to Rachel also, and his love for Rachel was greater than his love for Leah. And he worked for Laban another seven years.

(Genesis 29:27-30)

I have often wondered how Leah felt as she was veiled up and presented to Jacob during the wedding. How did she feel as Jacob lay with her that night knowing full well what would happen when it was morning? Did she agree to be used as such by her father to deceive Jacob?

I doubt if she had any say or much choice in the matter, to be given out to such a loveless marriage and rivalry with her sister for the rest of her life.

Although Jacob took care of Leah and provided for her, but he never loved her as he loved Rachel. Jacob loved Rachel more than Leah. God saw all that Jacob was doing to Leah and decided to shut Rachael's womb while He allowed Leah to have children. God blessed her womb, and these were her words she when her first three sons were born.

"The Lord has noticed my misery, and now my husband will love me." She named him Reuben: 'Behold a son!' (Genesis 29:32)

"The Lord heard that I was unloved and has given me another son." She said and named him Simeon which means 'Hearing' or 'That is heard' (Genesis 29:33). And still, Jacob didn't love her.

Leah was still seeking Jacob's love, her response to the birth of the third son reflected her pain: "Surely this time my husband will feel affection for me, since I have given him three sons!" She named him Levi meaning 'Attached' (Genesis 29:34).

She even had to give a gift to Rachael later in her marriage for Jacob to sleep with her (Genesis 30:14-16). If only you can imagine her pain of living with a husband who loved another and not her.

I know some of you have experienced or you're experiencing the pain of living with a spouse that does not love you. You're not alone in this. My husband loved me dearly before marriage just like Jacob loved Rachael but hated me with great passion after marriage like Jacob hated Leah. He sent me to his parents, like Leah was abandoned by Jacob, he abandoned me. But I have good news for you, just like God saw Leah's pain and favoured her with the fruit of the womb, He also favoured me with a male and a female, so all hope was not lost. You'll also find favour in the sight of God.

Leah, the unloved wife ultimately became the mother of six of Jacob's 12 sons. The names of her children were Reuben, Simeon, Levi, Judah Gen 30:16-17, Issachar, Zebulun, Dinah (Genesis 30:16-17). All the nations of the earth were blessed through her, for she gave birth to Levi, the ancestor of all the Jewish priests. Judah, also known as Praise (Genesis 49:8-12) was the ancestor of our Lord Jesus.

He got the highest blessing from Jacob - scepter (Royal authority and legal authority). He led Israel through the wilderness. He led the conquest of Canaan. He was the first tribe to praise David and made him King.

Leah never gained the affection of Jacob, yet her life was evidence of God's devotion to her. She lived with a husband who never loved her, she had no idea that the children she bore Jacob would make a great nation. Sometimes, it is hard to see positives when we're living through pain and crisis. We should always ask God to open our eyes to see beyond the pains we go through. God sees your situation and will be a refuge for you because He says, "I will show my love to the person who is not loved" (Hosea 2:23). Racheal died along the way and was buried beside the road to Bethlehem. But Leah, who also died before Jacob was buried in the cave of Patriarchs in Hebron alongside Abraham, Sarah, Isaac and Rebekkah and on his death bed Jacob commanded his sons to bury him beside Leah even though he died in Egypt - Gen 49:11

Do you feel unloved and unwanted, follow Leah's example of faithfulness to the end?

My story did not start as Leah's, but I do resonate with her being stuck in a loveless marriage despite all efforts to win the heart of her husband. My rivals unlike Leah are not my sister but other numerous women in my husband's life. To him, it was a thing of pride to date as many women as possible.

Despite the way he treated me, I was still a loving, caring, forward-thinking, hardworking, passionate, fun-loving, kind-hearted, patient; but how did these personalities impact my marriage? I went into marriage with an open heart,

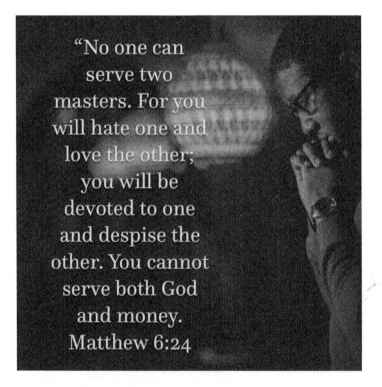

"No one can serve two masters. For you will hate one and love the other; you will be devoted to one and despise the other. You cannot serve both God and money. Matthew 6:24

• **A loving and caring wife**: My loving nature impacted my marriage. I was called Ruth Abókokú it means Ruth, the one that is too clingy, devoted, and loyal to her husband. I was always all over my husband. During our courtship, we were an item, always together as much as possible. As an undergraduate I did not get to go out to most of the social activities on campus, If I attended any, we were always together.

I enjoy cooking and particularly derived pleasure in cooking special meals for him.

• **Forward-thinking:** I tend not to cry over spilt milk. If something happens, I will naturally reflect on what has happened, where it went wrong and simply move on to find a solution instead of agonizing over the incident. My husband on the other hand was the complete opposite. He would fret and fret and get worried sick. Often this would lead to unnecessary quarrels as he would not let the sleeping dog lie. I guess this part of him had a huge negative impact on our marriage. He kept things to heart greatly and would not forgive easily.

Hardworking: I have never been lazy; I am generally a workaholic. Any time spent doing nothing seems to be wasted. I always love to get busy doing one thing or the other. I was raised to be independent, and naturally, I am entrepreneurial. So, I would take risks, venture into the unknowns, and work it out along the way. Sometimes it worked well, other times I failed, but then

I don't let this weigh me down. I get up from where I've fallen and continue the race.

•**A passionate individual:** I commit my all to whatever I do. I carry out all activities wholeheartedly. There's is no sitting on the fence, it's either I am in or out. I enjoy learning new things.

•**Fun-loving**: I try as much as possible to make every single moment a pleasurable and a memorable one. I often turn simple tasks into fun time, makes jokes and do have a good laugh even at my own gaffs. I see each day as a gift to be treasured, so I make the most of each moment. I also love taking pictures. Amongst my friends and colleagues, I am the un-official paparazzi who liven up events.

•**Kind-hearted**: I am my brother's keeper. I do not like to see anyone suffer. I do everything within my power to help ease any one's pain or suffering even when it's to my detriment. I take risks a lot for people until I became wiser and tougher and learned to spot the difference, as there a saying "there comes a time when you have to stop crossing ocean for people who wouldn't even cross puddle for you".

•**A patient being**: Due to my patient nature, I'm often taken for granted. But like I always say to myself, patience is not a weakness, it's a virtue.

•**A no-nonsense individual**: Although I tend to have long-suffering, I also do not take rubbish from people. I will firmly stand my ground on any issue I strongly believe in. Sometimes my husband took my patient trait for granted and until I react, it surprised him that I stood my ground.

My Little Support

One of the good things I did in my marriage was helping to put food on the table when there was none. During my course of my undergraduate studies, I will engage in sales of small chops and drinks whenever lecturers in my school go on a long strike due to poor working conditions. During this long period of strike, things could be difficult and sometimes there was no food for any member of the family. Sometimes my husband will leave the house and go to play snooker with his friends who were students. He would return home to a nice dinner and wondered how I managed to prepare the meal. This puts smiles on my face. My sister and I would make chin. Chin (a snack) and kunnu (a drink), take them to the kiosks around for sale. I would go back to the kiosks in the evening to get the proceeds from the sales. I am an industrious and hardworking woman and would do any legal task to put food on our table. (I had my son and two of my ex-husbands brother's living with us at the time I went back to the university for my final year).

Living with my In-laws

My husband felt it was better I stay with his parents because my pregnancy had advanced. Hence, I lived with my in-laws in the early years of my marriage. Most times I wonder why he wouldn't stay with me in his parents' house. We had a 3-bedroom flat in Oru (a smaller town between Ago-Iwoye and Ijebu-Igbo) which is just about seven miles from where his parents lived. He could stay with me and go to work from there; but he chose to stay in Oru and come at weekends. Sometimes he comes home on Saturday.

My parents -in law were very kind and gracious to me, especially my father-in-law. Although he was a disciplinarian whose bark was worse than his bit.

However, he had such a kind heart, that he would move mountains if necessary to make sure no harm came the way of his loved ones. I remember when I was sick with chickenpox which led to my miscarriage, and I was isolated in a room downstairs in the family apartment. The family doctor came to administer drugs to me morning and night and change the IV drips I was on. My father-in-law regularly came in to check on me to see how I was. As I got better, he would stay with me, watch me eat and make sure I took my medications. I was taken to the hospital by my father-in-law when I went into labour. He stayed with me through the night until I gave birth to my first child, and he was also with me when I had my second child.

My mother-in-law was a diamond. When I had my first son, she took care of everything. The only thing I was allowed to do was to breastfeed my baby. She would get off her bed very early, come to my apartment, bathe, and watch me feed my son. She would give me the hot water afterbirth steaming and massage my belly for it to return to its pre-pregnancy form.

The steaming was quite a painful and memorable experience. My son was very big for a first pregnancy. My doctor had jokingly said he lived in a room and parlour while in my belly (that he had a lot of room to grow in) and so I had a very deep episiotomy. As traditionally done for women, I had to sit over a pot of steam with antiseptic for it to speed up the healing and to prevent infection. But in my case, some of the stitches came loose and when I went for my regular post-natal checkup, they had to scrape it to create a fresh wound and restitched it. Becoming a mother can be very challenging.

When the ASUU strike eventually ended, I resumed back to school; It was my final year and I had moved back to the flat. Initially, I would leave my son with my mother-in-law but later pleaded with my husband to allow my son to stay with us. My son's presence gave me so much peace of mind and sanity. My son stayed with us 'till it was time for me to go for the mandatory NYSC (National Youth Service Corps). Although I schooled in a university close to Lagos State, to my surprise, I was posted to Lagos. This shouldn't have been so by the rules governing the program.

You would usually get such redeployment when you have connections in the right places, which I don't have. Another blessing in disguise.

The period between January to August in 1998, while I was waiting for my NYSC posting, was the hardest for me. As I was slowly losing my mind. I was already pregnant with my second child, and this made my mother-in-law kick against my going to serve because I was five months pregnant; but I still went.

I had a bet with my father-in-law to deliver a girl but predicted that I'm going to give birth to a boy. My father-in-law took me to the hospital during my second labour and I delivered a baby girl. I won the bet, and he did redeem his pledge.

After my maternity leave, I moved back to Lagos to continue my youth service. Initially, my husband would visit the children and I every other weekend, but sometimes three weeks or a month interval between visits. **Like Leah, he abandoned me.** He stopped doing a whole lot of things he used to do before we got married, he stopped being affectionate and he visited us in Lagos less frequently.

Overtime, with the relationship breaking down, it became worse to a point it seems we were no longer together. However, at some point, our relationship appeared to be on the mend. it was then he decided to relocate to the UK and the family joined him a few years later.

CHAPTER THREE

UNCOMSUMMATED MARRIAGE

CHAPTER THREE

UNCOMSUMMATED MARRIAGE

Marriage is honourable, and pleasurable in the sight of God. Hence sexual intercourse in marriage is a tripartite fusion of the spirit, soul and body. It is the binding factor that **makes the two blood and souls come together** and become one soul and one blood. It is a tie that binds two souls together in love and unity. It is a fellowship at the deepest level that is beyond the physical, each partner gives a part of themselves to each other (one of the major reasons it is dangerous to have multiple sex partners). The purpose of sexual intimacy in marriage is two-fold. Firstly, for pleasure and communion and secondly for procreation. Most marriages and societies only take sexual intercourse to be for procreation and nothing more. This is a fallacy because children are a gift from God, conception is not determined by the number of times sexual intercourse occur (as most pregnancies occur when you least expect).

Another fallacy in marriage and society is that the woman is being considered with less affection once the

union has produced children. A married woman is treated like a common commodity as soon as she's able to reproduce. Her husband no longer cherishes and pamper her as he does before procreation. The level of sexual intimacy also reduces drastically with time, and some feel their spouses do not need regular sex anymore.

How should Sexual intercourse between a man and his wife be?

> *And they were both naked, the man and his wife, and were not ashamed, KJV (Genesis 2:25).*

Most people get married in their prime, when they are still young and very attractive. But as they get older, they seem to become less attractive. This is very obvious in most women who add more weight after childbirth and also in men that develop protruding stomachs after they get married. The husband and wife become too familiar for optimum sex and oftentimes harbour resentment about the changes that have occurred in the physical body. This ought not to be so, mutual attraction should exist between couples. Each partner should love one another purely and always see one another as attractive because the soul is the real personality of the person. We are created in God's image; we are a reflection of His beauty and glory. Our real self is our soul and our soul lives in a body – our physical body and it ages until it eventually dies but our soul is ageless, it lives on. Therefore, the physical body should not be the binding factor, rather both partners should be connected by the soul.

Some couples don't see sexual intercourse as a sacrament or a holy mystery. They think there are a lot more to marriage than sex and hence sex seems like a chore to them or a mere performance of marital duties. Although we are all wired differently, each person in a relationship should study their partner, learn and understand each other's love language and create no room for boredom even as the marriage is a long-term commitment. When you take time to understand your partner, sexual intimacy gets better and become more satisfying because you know each other's likes, dislikes, and preferences.

Sex is a journey that has a beginning and an end, along the way it has its twists and curves highs and lows. It could be spontaneous or planned. My ex-husband used to tell me that sex is a thing of the mind and until much later did I come to understand this phrase. Sex is a natural human desire that does not just involve the body but also involve emotions and moods. There must be a mind-body connection for good sex to occur. The environment and personal hygiene are also a major factor in making sexual intercourse pleasurable and enjoyable.

Applying The 3 Steps to enjoying
Marital Sex

Escape the no sex marriage

What do you do before having sexual intercourse?

Before having sex, you should get into the mood so you can get into your groove. Develop sexy thoughts in your head and think about what's erotic to you i.e., what's going to turn you on.

Keep your mind focused by finishing all your to-do lists. You should also give your partner a clue into your pre-romp excitement. Send your partner love/erotic messages, check out a sexual position you've not tried out yet, download the picture and send it to your partner to arouse him/her sexually. Stay away from food that causes bloating or bad breath, Prepare or order a nice meal. Have a bath/ shower, apply scents, reach out for an outfit that will make you feel sexy or get you in the mood. Slip into your sexual skivvies that makes you feel confident. Set the environment for a pleasant time together depending on your personal circumstances.

Some of the things to do during sex

During sexual intercourse, be eager to discover your partner's pleasure points, be adventurous. Trace their lips slowly with your tongue and kiss. Get your partner closer to orgasm by licking their ear and whispering something like: how do you feel when I touch you? Do not be ashamed to exploring your partner. Kiss the back of his neck slightly with your mouth or run/massage his hairline with your fingertips. Explore his erogenous zones by playing on one of his nipples. You can also try something new by giving a dirty talk a whirl.

What to do after sex

There are two aftermaths of sexual intercourse. The first aftermath is the climax itself, the peak of the release of emotions. This usually happens when you reach the height of sexual arousal. The sexual tension in your body increases until it reaches a peak and then the pressure in your body and finally the genital is released of the pressure. After orgasm, don't be selfish, instead, seek your partner's pleasurable release. The second aftermath of sexual intercourse is cuddling up and talking sweet nothings. Have a pillow talk with your partner, this is a safe, genuine and loving communication and connection that occur in bed or while cuddling. It allows you to speak more unconsciously. It is the best time to discuss and settle issues, make plans, and reach agreements. It also increases the love for each other, it helps you feel closer and connected to your partner and foster the feelings of being loved.

Sexual Enhancement

Sexual enhancement is a substance that arouses or increases sexual desire, sexual attraction, sexual pleasure, or sexual behaviour. I found a sexual enhancement drug in one of my husband's bags. By this time, we were all in the UK. You may be thinking he's finding it difficult to give me sexual satisfaction and so decides to use aphrodisiac to improve his sexual performance as a married man and not deny me my marital rights. If this is what you're thinking, then you're wrong because my husband had the aphrodisiac for another purpose.

One fateful day, I called in sick and decided to stay in bed the whole day because I was indisposed. I slept for a while and then picked up a book to read a few minutes after I woke up. As I was reading, I had the urge to check a bag in the wardrobe. I ignored the urge and continued reading but the urge kept prompting me and I finally decided to check the bag in the wardrobe to have peace from the voice prompting me repeatedly. I was amazed by what I found in the bag. I found some sex enhancement drugs in it, and some had been used. I wondered why my husband had them in his bag.

He hadn't touched me nor had sex with me in many months and each time I ventured near him I was always rebuffed. Most nights, he sleeps in such a way that makes it difficult for me to come closer to him.

When he came back home from work that night, I welcomed him warmly and served him his meal. Later that night when we retire to bed, I handed him the pack of stimulants I found and a glass of water. I asked him to take the drugs after which we could have sex. He became very angry and enraged. He raised his voice at me and asked what audacity I had to check his bag or even go through his things. He kept throwing questions at me angrily. As the barrage of words came at me, I told him I found the stimulants accidentally and decided to give them to him that night since he always complained of tiredness. I asked him why he had them in his possession if it was not to improve his sexual performance with me. My questions sounded irritating and rhetorical. He didn't give a response rather, he covered himself up with the duvet and slept off. I was confused and hurt. Why would my husband take aphrodisiac and still deny me sex? I realised my husband has been unfaithful to me repeatedly hence an explanation for some of the tablets that had been used.

I wept in silence and cried so hard that night. The pillow became soggy with tears and finally, I fell asleep.

> COME TO THE EDGE," HE SAID.
> "WE CAN'T, WE'RE AFRAID!" THEY
> RESPONDED.
> "COME TO THE EDGE," HE SAID.
> "WE CAN'T, WE WILL FALL!" THEY
> RESPONDED.
> "COME TO THE EDGE," HE SAID.
> AND SO THEY CAME.
> AND HE PUSHED THEM.
> AND THEY FLEW."
>
> - GUILLAUME APOLLINAIRE

Now I have realised that my husband's infidelity days are not over. I was just as much in danger as prostitutes, if not more, from getting hit with STDs. I mean, sleeping with a serial cheat wasn't going to do my health any favours. But I was luckier than hurt.

I had flash back memories of when we were in Nigeria having suffered discomfort after discomfort. It got to a point my GP ran a HIV test unbeknownst to me. Only when it turned out negative did he disclose the series of tests carried out. I was doubly scared and grateful. You see, God Himself created sexual instincts, to be explored within the confines of marriage. If you read the book of

Solomon, sexual union and its pleasure have been aptly described. When it comes to sex in marriage and issues surrounding positions, oral sex and sex toys, I believe there are three main guiding principles:

1. Does the scripture prohibit it?

2. Is it harmful or helpful?

3. Is it mutual consent?

Solomon 2:13, 4:16, 1 Cor 6:12, 7:5

Are other bedroom activities bringing you together or increasing you further apart? When I found these drugs, he was preparing for his trip to Nigeria. However, I took a photo and reported him to my uncle. He had always mediated our marital issues. My uncle

promised to have a talk with my husband once he returned from his trip. As usual, on his arrival he bought lots of gifts and stuff for his family in Nigeria. I watched as the parcels arrived, but I didn't say anything. What I did not realise was that bitterness and anger was gaining deep roots in my heart.

He travelled leaving us without even so much as a dime for our needs. The night he left, I was in such state of bitterness, utter rage. I was murderous. An evil thought crept into my heart - Oh how I wish his plane crashed into the deep ocean, so he would never come back, and I would be free of this torture. Argh! ... Immediately I was rebuked, and I knelt, weeping and praying to God for mercy and forgiveness. How and when did I become this? *A murderer???* God help me... Because I was hurting, I was now wishing to kill three hundred other passengers because one person onboard!!! Lord have mercy!!! Dear readers, if your marriage is anything like mine, not working after all attempts, draining your sanity, and turning you into a murderer... PLEASE LEAVE. EMOTIONAL damage is not visible, but it's a deep, silent killer...

> *Proverb 25:28 says, "Like a city whose walls are broken down is a man who lacks self-control." In other words, if we do not control our own lives from the inside, somebody else will control them from the outside"*
>
> *Myles Munroe*

CHAPTER FOUR

TOXIC MARRIAGE RELATIONSHIP

CHAPTER FOUR

TOXIC MARRIAGE RELATIONSHIP

Five Weeks of Hell

Prior to the miscarriage, I had a lot going on in my life. Somehow, I had always been afraid of my 32nd birthday and as it approached, I intensified my prayers......little did I know what was in stock for me, but for the saving grace and mercy of God, He saw me through. The revelation gave direction to my prayers and God intervened in the situation by saving me from death and preserving my life. The generational yoke was finally broken. I remembered God's promises in His word *"He who dwells in the secret place of the most high shall abide under the shadow of the Almighty. I will say of the Lord, he Is my refuge and fortress: My God: in him will I trust" (Psalm 91:1-2). No doubt, God is my refuge and fortress.*

I would share a bit of what transpired. God is merciful and gracious, He vindicated me in so many ways. I will share a few of my experiences with you.

Suspension Saga

One of my colleagues at work was reprimanded for her addictive habit of going to the hairdressers weekly during work hours. The matter could easily have been resolved amicably but my colleague reported to the head office because she was highly connected. She indicted me and another colleague of mine, that we both went with her to the hairdressers. We were summoned to the head office to defend ourselves. My other colleague and I fasted and prayed for God's mercy, favour and intervention. After this spiritual activity, the case was closed with just a slap on the wrist instead of suspension.

Car Fire incident

God also saved me from a fire care accident. One fateful day, on a Monday morning, my cousin decided to drive me to my place of work in Victoria Island, Lagos. I noticed white smoke around us as soon as we came off the third mainland bridge in Ikoyi. I assumed the white smoke was coming out of the car next to us. The fume kept increasing and I instructed my cousin to park the car at a safe spot to examine it. We discovered the smoke was coming out from the bonnet of my car. I knew something isn't working properly and there was some damage to my car engine or exhaust system. My cousin decided to open the bonnet of the car to examine if there was some damage to the car engine or exhaust. As soon as he opened the bonnet, the car burst into flames and caught fire. I was shocked and stood at a safe spot for minutes and watched the car burn. Several thoughts ran through my mind, I'd filled the tank with 75 litres of petrol the previous night. I was so full of gratitude to God. I wouldn't want to imagine the scary incident of being trapped in a burning car whilst the car is in motion in the third mainland bridge which is the longest in Nigeria (with a total length of 11.8 Km).

Varicella-zoster infection (ill-treatment from husband despite miscarriage)

The fire incident happened a few days before I travelled to London for holiday. I started feeling ill two days before my travelling scheduled date, so I called my travelling agent to cancel my flights. I don't like taking drugs or any form of medication because I found most medicine has an awful taste and even a choking smell.

But when it's becoming a case of life and death, I'll have no choice but to see a doctor. I also called my husband to inform him I will be coming over to see him so he could take me to the family hospital as I preferred our family doctor to see me when I'm seriously ill.

I boarded a bus going to Ijebu-Igbo and alighted at Oru, a small town along the route. I was in pain all through the journey, my whole body was burning up with a fever and my belly hurt badly with cramps. I held back the pain and fought back tears from **running down my eyes**. As I got closer to where I will alight, I called my husband to please come to the bus stop to wait for me. I spotted my husband standing at the bus stop as I came out from the bus and started to walk towards him in pain. I expected my husband to walk towards me at least to give me support while I walked but instead, he ignored me and walked on ahead to where he had parked his car over a distance. Anyone seeing us as we walk apart would never have imagined that we were together. Although I'm a softie that would cry along with another person when they are in pain or going through unbear- able circumstances especially when watching a movie, yet I have a high threshold for pain and find it difficult to shed tears from physical pain. Although anybody in my shoes would have probably filled a bucket with tears. I could barely walk and each step I took became heavier and all my husband did was watch me from his car where he sat. When I finally got to the car, he zoomed off and drove me home to his place. I realised he had no inten- tion of taking me to the hospital, I insisted I wouldn't sleep in his house that night without being examined by the doctor. He argued he couldn't drive well at night but after much persistence from me, he eventually drove me to his cousin's clinic in Ijebu Ode. When I got to the clinic, I was treated for malaria and asked to come back the next day. I complained about a few spots I noticed on my arms and face, but the doctor asked me to take my drugs as prescribed and observe if there'll be any changes.

When I got back home that night, I noticed I was bleeding but assumed it was my monthly flow although it was very painful with clumps. I felt weak and dizzy and had cramps in my stomach. It was as if a dog was running around in circles chasing its tail. I screamed in pain as I went for my bed. I felt an awful, it was like I was being kicked in the stomach. The cramp soon subsided, and I fell asleep. The next morning, I had more of those small, fluid-filled blisters all over my body and they were itchy. My husband called in our family GP who examined me when he arrived and immediately placed me on admission with Intravenous drips as I refused to be admitted to the clinic. The doctor told me I had chickenpox and had miscarried. I was so devastated because I had been trying to have another baby and had not even realised I was pregnant. I felt very uncomfortable about the miscarriage, it was like I was unjustified because I never met my baby girl/boy. I grieved and mourned my loss. I felt devasted and wondered why I would carry a perfectly healthy fetus then after a few weeks, lose the fetus. I became intensely sad and felt empty.

I was under medical care and admission at home for four days. My father-in-law kept watch over me, but hubby returned to his base and came back two days later. My doctor advised me he would carry out an evacuation and clear out the remaining fetus when I recover fully as I was very weak. On the 5th day when I felt better, I went back to Lagos and returned to Ijebu a week after for the evacuation. I was driven to the clinic by my cousin who waited while I undergo the procedure. The evacuation process was painful, I screamed and wept profusely until the process was over. I cried for the loss of my baby and also for the pain of a broken heart as I struggled to understand why my hubby was ignoring me and did not care about what I was going through. My husband arrived at the clinic after the evacuation process was over and the doctor had to tell him off.

After I was discharged, my cousin drove me to Lagos. I researched the effects of chickenpox during early pregnancy and discovered it could lead to low birth weight and limb abnormalities but in my case, I had a miscarriage and lost the baby. God who knows the end from the beginning new that having a miscarriage was a lesser burden than going through nine months of pregnancy abandoned and later had to deal with complications with my baby.

The Burglars

As I was recovering from the evacuation of the fetus and the chicken pox infection, I was with my children in the living room watching the television. My husband's cousin who lived with us, went out to buy some insecticide spray but did not lock the door properly instead she just closed the mosquito netting door when she came back home. As we watched -Super Story- a Nigerian soap opera, ironically, the scene was a robbery scene. I heard a strange voice "Good evening, everybody, we are armed robbers everyone lie down flat". I'd so much fixed my gaze on the television that I didn't react to the voice. I did not know when the strange figures walked in until, I felt a cold metal being pressed on my cheek and a stern voice ordering me to cooperate or I would be wasted.

They ordered me to my bedroom and robbed me of my jewelry, I had a lot of them as I believed they were a form of investment. Their leader ransacked everywhere for money and when he wouldn't find any, he hit my face and asked where I kept my money. I told him it was in my handbag in the living room. When we got to the living room, he checked my bag and found nothing. He was enraged and threatened to kill me with his gun if I don't tell him where I kept my money. I became bold all of a sudden and told him that one of his boys had searched the bag and taken the money because I had fifty thousand naira in the bag and that couldn't he see the bag had ben upturned. All through this ordeal, I was praying under my breath to God to save me and my family and God answered by causing confusion in their midst. An argument broke out amongst them as they argued over the money and jewelry until one of them who was outside cautioned them about making a lot of noise and wasting so much time. They searched the living room and went away with anything that caught their attention. They finally left but after they've succeeded in locking me and my children in the bathroom. We remained quiet for a while and when we were sure they'd left, we shouted for help and was rescued by one of our neighbours. My children were so traumatised for many days and refused to sleep in their room.

Home Fire Incident

A few days after the robbery incident, I went into the kitchen to check on my husband's cousin who was cooking beans on the stove. I noticed she placed the stove on the floor in an awkward position close to the door and asked her to move the stove to a safer position to allow easy opening and closing of the kitchen door. She brought down the pot from the stove and dragged the stove on the floor. As she dragged the stove, the stove overturned, and the kerosene poured out and immediately the kitchen caught fire. She and I rushed out of the building then I heard my children crying as they were trapped in the living room. There was no way for them to get out as the door in the living room was permanently shut and the kitchen door was the only entry and exit to the house. I was still very weak and was yet to recover from the illness I had so I could do nothing but pray to God for a miracle and His intervention.

As I stood watching the burning kitchen, I remembered a testimony someone had shared about a fire Incident in her house. She had grabbed her tithe record book and used it as a fan to blow out the fire and miraculously the fire went out. I also started praying to God to intervene and remember my faithfulness in my tithing and save my children from the fire incident. All my neighbours came out of their apartments, some with detergents and others with buckets of water, they added the detergents into the water and douse the raging kitchen fire with the mixture. The whole saga lasted for a few minutes and the fire was eventually put out. The fire had burnt even the ceiling and the smoke was very thick. One of my neighbours rushed inside the house and brought out my children.

I was indebtedly grateful to God for his everlasting mercy that saw me through my trying period. Although the enemies waged war against me and came like a flood, but the spirit of God lifted a standard against them. My God who never sleeps nor slumbers was faithfully watching over me and my household.

CHAPTER FIVE

PHILANDERER

CHAPTER FIVE

PHILANDERER

Infidelity in Marriage

Ever since I found an aphrodisiac in my husband's bag, I've always questioned myself why would my husband be having extramarital affairs? What could have made my husband infidelious? I had several questions on my mind, is cheating truly a man's nature? Is my husband a philander because we're not living together since we got married or is he exposed to temptations he couldn't resist in his place of work? Is he having extramarital affairs because his religion support marrying more than one wife? Even if the answers to all my questions was a yes, they're not enough reasons to justify a married man engaging in adultery, of the, opined that whatsoever a man does is out of his own will and choice, and nothing is enough justification except when it's willingly done.

As humans, we make different choices daily, from simple choices to complex ones. For example, we get to choose what to eat, drink, wear, read, attend to or not. We choose the places we want to go to or not to, we choose to go to bed early or stay up late. We decide if we want to study a course, language, technique or not. If we want to travel or not, date a particular person or not. Each choice we make have its reward and consequences.

Over the years I reflected on the problems in my marriage. I have given it a thought, what has gone wrong in my marriage. How did we end up in this mess? Where did we get it wrong? Was it my fault or his? Did my husband intentionally become a philander because his religion supports him having many wives or he was not just aware of its implications on our marriage?

I began to have a clearer picture of my husband's past actions. Now I understood why he asked me to live with his parents in my advanced stage of pregnancy and wouldn't allow me returned to our apartment three months after I had my baby. I lived with my in-laws for 18 months because of my IT that was extended to almost two years due to the ASUU strike. My husband could have commuted to work daily as the distance from his parent's house to his place of work was only 30mins

drive. But instead, he chose to come home only on Friday evenings and sometimes he wouldn't come home until Saturday afternoon and then leave very early on Monday morning.

I wouldn't have agreed to the idea of me living with his parents if we'd discussed it before marriage since we had our apartment. I felt like he married me to please his parents who were concerned for his safety and wanted him to settle down early because of his lifestyle. He obeyed his parent's instructions, became a married man, took his wife to live with them and went off to continue living the lifestyle he wanted. In one of the books written by Kate Iroegbu, the transformational and sensational writer, **titled "Marriage is to be enjoyed not endured", stated that "marriage is not meant for every-one" and I agree** to this.

My husband had a lot of sexual escapades, I will share with you the last straw that finally broke the camel's back.

My mother-in-law who is a typical Nigerian mum had started pressuring me to have more children, she would ask "Do you want to have only two children" at every opportunity she got. My husband comes home on some weekends, so this fateful week was my fertile period as I just finished menstruating a few days back. I purchased a fertility boosting supplement from a pharmacy with Onye my dear friend who also has the same quest as mine to get pregnant. I was happy and excited about my husband coming home that weekend and had taken the fertility boosting supplement as prescribed by the pharmacist. But then I received the bad news, my husband rang to say he would not be coming home that weekend. I felt disappointed, pained and upset thinking I'd so much prepared for his coming only to have all plans ruined by him not coming home. I was uncomfortable throughout the weekend due to the supplements I've taken. I felt so much discomforts as it seems my ovaries were releasing eggs in tons and were bubbling over and over just like the way a cooking porridge boils, now am beginning to have the feeling that conception would have ended up being a twin pregnancy, you needed to hear the rock and roll bubbling taking place in my ovaries that weekend. Shared my experience with a friend when I saw her at work the next Monday morning. Although we were disappointed our plans failed, we laughed out loud for a few minutes. Fortunately for my friend, she lives together with her husband. Her case was different and not as mine. She later conceived and gave birth to twin babies. Children are indeed the heritage of the Lord, and the fruit of the womb is its reward. Although one can plan and wish, man proposes but God disposes.

On a different occasion, during my fertile period of the month, so I decided to spend an amorous weekend with my husband with the hope of conceiving. My cousin who was home with my children will take good care of them. I didn't resume work on Friday morning, instead, I picked up my already packed bag and drove off to Oru town to be with my husband. As I approached the house, I could see my husband and the landlord's son who was his friend standing outside and washing their cars.

I got down from the car and exchanged pleasantries with the landlord's son, my husband immediately left what he was doing and walked straight inside the house. I was dumbfounded because he didn't say hello to me nor respond when I greeted him. The landlord's son tried to engage me in a lengthy conversation in a bid to keep me waiting outside. I got the clue something is amiss, so I politely ended the conversation then walked inside to meet my husband. I was shocked by what I saw when I got into the house, my husband hurriedly threw the small suitcase of clothes he was carrying across the adjoining corridor to the apartment of his friend. I walked into the house and quietly sat down on the chair in the living room.

My husband was pacing up and down the house looking very restless. I soon walked to the toilet to urinate. While still using the rest room, I noticed an odd sight, there was a towel spread over a bucket and I assumed it must have fallen off the clothing rail. I picked it up intending to place it in its appropriate place and was taken aback by what I saw in the bucket. The bucket contained a lot of female undies. Whosoever put them there but had done so hurriedly and covered it with the towel. I picked one of the panties and tucked it into my skirt and covered the bucket with the towel just as it was. I walked back to the living room enraged and sat on a chair. "Why did you come unannounced? my husband asked as he stared angrily at me. " Do I need an invitation to come to my husband? I snapped back at him. He walked out of the room and went back to washing his car.

As he got out of sight, I walked to the other apartment to find out what he was hiding from me. No sooner had I begun the search I found a young girl in her early twenties sitting in his friends living room. As I beheld her, I thought of beating the living daylight out of her but decided she wasn't worth the trouble.

I took my last glance at her and walked back to my husband's house. My husband had finished whatsoever he was doing, probably loading her belongings into his car and walked up to me and asked if I took anything. "What are you looking for? I walked into the house with just my car keys I replied to him. For reasons best known to him he couldn't tell me one of the undies belonging to his concubine is missing and if I'd seen it. After a few minutes of pacing around and uneasiness, he told me he needed to drop off something for someone and will be back shortly.

As I watched him leave, I felt up in arms but didn't utter a word because I was seriously bubbling inside of me and would have erupted violently like a volcano if I had opened my mouth to say anything or stood up from the chair, this would have caused massive disaster. It was a case of adding insult to injury as a crushing pain seared through my chest. A flood of aches and pain broke out in my soul; I felt stung, (after he had left) I exhaled severally and took several deep breaths to calm me down and then walked into my car and drove off to Ijebu-ode letting tears flow down my face.

The drive which is just about 15 minutes seems like an eternity. His concubine must have been very important to him because he chose to leave me sitting in the living room and go drop her at her destination.

The Effect on Me

I was about losing my mind and decided to park the car and walk around to ease my worries as I could be involved in an accident if I drive on with my unstable frame of mind. I got down from the car and walked aimlessly towards the heart of the market, head down and shoulder bowed not sure which way I was going or what direction to take. I had a terrifying feeling that I was slowly losing control of myself, and if I let go, I would go insane, (In Nigeria, insanity is deemed incurable and at its peak when the victim is seen roaming the marketplace).

After walking aimlessly for a few minutes, I felt sufficiently calm and walked back to my car to continue my journey. I received a call from my father-in-law as soon as I got home asking about my whereabouts.

My husband had gone to his parent's house to look for me when he didn't meet me at home only to find out I had returned to my base to continue my single life in marriage. He must have also told them what transpired between us including the fact that I had taken the girls knickers because my father-in-law had asked for an explanation and reasons for my actions. I narrated the ordeal to him and told him I took the items only as evidence of my husband's infidelity. My father-in-law pleaded with me to return the items to my husband since he was sure I had no bad intention of taking it in the first place. I agreed to return the knickers to my husband and ended the call. I was still writhing in agony like a fish on a hook, slowly and did not explain to my beloved children the reason I came back earlier than expected.

I thought my ordeals were over until my husband came home that evening looking fierce as a bear with a sore head. I assumed he wanted to apologize to me for his unfaithfulness and arrogance, but my assumption was wrong. I was hauled over the coal for coming to his house without giving his prior notice and also for taking the knicker. Don't you know you'll be the first suspect if anything happens to that girl, he lashed out at me as if I've been fetish all my life? As he talked the hind leg off a donkey, I cried and handed the items to him as soon as he finished talking. As the Lord who I serve lives, the humiliations, heartache, pains and sorrow I suffered today because of that girl today will be multiplied in hundredfold and will be her portion and her generations unborn, they would never know any form of peace or joy in marriage.

I cursed bitterly as he walked away with the item. He walked out of the house unremorsefully and didn't come home for several weeks. My broken heart continued to bleed from the pain, neglect, rejection, abandonment, maltreatment etc.

I suffered heartache for several weeks. My heart felt shattered, and I cried myself to sleep every night. The sheer weight of the hurt pulled me down and dragged me into the deep dark abyss. I couldn't stop it; I couldn't prevent it.

All I could do is cry, until one midnight after crying my heart out, I looked out through the window into the clear midnight sky and sat down, seated curled up in a fetal position. As the soft moonlight bathed my room from the window, I sat on the floor of my bedroom and rocked myself back and forth, lost in my pain and from that moment I decided never to allow anyone to hurt me again. As no human being should have the capability to hurt another this much. Evil is real, there is wickedness and there is WICKEDNESS. I was badly hurt because I love deeply, I no longer need a heart. I'm strong, I'm a warrior, nobody can hurt me without my permission I said to myself.

So, I mentally visualised yanking out my shattered heart, packing up every piece of it into a bag and flung it into outer space to be floating amongst the galaxies and stars where no human can reach it and hurt me ever again and determined to live by it. I got up from the floor reborn, went to the bathroom to wash my face after which I climbed onto my bed and slept. I slept like a baby; it was the best night sleep I've ever had in many months.

The old weakling Debbie died and was buried. I was prepared physically, mentally and emotionally ready to enter a new chapter in my life.

CHAPTER SIX

THE LETTER FROM THE MAN I LOVED

CHAPTER SIX

THE LETTER FROM THE MAN I LOVED

He practically worshipped the ground I walked on – before marriage.

He was a very brilliant man who would deliver lectures without referring to any notebooks. The same topic taught in separate classes would be different. And his courses where not one of the easiest - think about those complex mathematics - but he had his unique way of teaching and making everything seamless. One of the things he said that attracted me to him was my intelligence. He said he could never marry an *olodo* (dullard). And so, he took keen interest in my academic progress, forcing me to study hard and weaning me off my rather lackadaisical attitude towards studying – piling everything up till last minute of exams instead of preparing way in advance.

As for looks, he was a very handsome man, with pink lips and a nicely set sparkly white teeth combining to make him *that* dashing man ladies sought after.

His hair, so thick and curly my favourite past time was to run my fingers through it especially when wet, really nice, soft and curly. He took great pride in his appearance and paid much attention to his looks. I remember a time I wanted to have a haircut and he chose the Toni Braxton short hair style...wow....it really suited me, and I could easily have passed for Toni herself.

He also had a great dress sense and routinely donned top designer outfits and cologne. I often jokingly said he bathed in it. His scent filled the air long before his entrance and continued to rent the room long after his exit. Often, he would take me shopping and pick out lovely items for me, such that anytime I wore an outfit he bought for me, I had heads turning in admiration as I walked past. I remember him buying me my first pair of jeans and I did not want to wear it outside of the house, but he insisted. I would say I felt uncomfortable as it brought out my hourglass figure and drew attention I did not want. But he would have none of it... He just simply took pride in showing me off.

Dancing is another great skill; he is very agile on his feet and a great dancer. We both share a love for music and dancing. He was particularly good at the choice of the music selections and would have been a great DJ if he had chosen to follow that path. I often encouraged him to do so as a part time hobby, but he always declined. His music compilation was superb. My flat mates always look forward to the times I was in my flat because of the music I would be blasting away, all selected and compiled by my ex-husband. We spent most evenings laying together listening to music, talking sweet nothings.

We would go to the market together, cook together, do the laundry together - my only task was to rinse and air dry while he did the actual washing. I couldn't iron any item properly even if my life depended on it, but he was dead good at it and would gladly take on the task. Almost therapeutic for him, he could spend minutes on end ironing one item. He gladly sorted the laundry while I aired and folded them away. He showered me with so much love and affection, I felt like a queen.

Since he had no car then, we hailed a private car everywhere we went. All he wanted was the best for the queen of his heart, me, Debbie. I felt special, protected and loved. He could not bear me out of his sight for longer than necessary and always kept me out of harm's way.

- Snippet of one of the letters below:

10:10pm
Tuesday 26th of September 1995.

"Darling, believe it or not, I am not at all in a very good mood tonight. In fact, right now I feel so downhearted and in tears for an unfounded reason. But I feel something so important in my life is nowhere to be found. And that thing is you Debbie, I wanted to remember all your promises. Part in the letter when I was in Italy, and some said at one time or the other. I wouldn't want it to make me feel as if the letter writing was out of infatuation.

However, darling I want to assure you once again, of my sincere love for you. I want you to know that the love I have for you, is nothing but real love. And nothing's gonna change my love for you. But what about you, Debbie, you know how scary I feel. Whenever you're in Lagos. It isn't that I don't trust or believe in you. But as you know, that is a self-assurance, much as so much in a relationship, especially in a situation where distances making things a little difficult....

Darling, know that the key to my success in life and happiness is you and God and that you're holding my heart and please treat it as gentle as possible so that it doesn't drop from your hand. And always remember that I'm here waiting for you, as no one can take your place. You mean the world to me, and I will always cherish your love for me how I wish by now that there shouldn't be any doubt in your mind, about my love and seriousness I promise you happiness, or you will never regret falling in love with me.. I'm not religious, but I believe in the power of God. So, whatever your doubts are, I believe God will definitely do the best"

I stumbled on the above letter whilst going through some files. I showed it to my children, who could not believe those were words from their dad but for his handwriting and obvious paper colour change to a brownish hue over time.

However, having read about the man I courted and the man I was married to, what could you imagine caused such a drastic change in one man? What happened to us? What turned my knight in shining armour to my tormentor? Where did we lose it all?

Three key things make or mar any relationship - sex, communication, and money.

SEX

My ex went from a man who got turned on just by being close to me, to someone irritated at the thought of standing in the same room. Our intimacy went down south as my first pregnancy advanced, dying a slow death and finally ending after the fight over enhancement drugs. And for the six years before I finally moved out, we had no intimacy.

COMMUNICATION

This followed the same pattern. From lying in bed whispering sweet nothings to each other, talking about the future, to exchanging nasty, terrible, and hurtful words, and finally staying aloof from each other for almost two years all the while sharing the same house and same bed? Yes, it was torturing, but God saw me through. Sadly, many women are stuck in this prison, enduring for years on end emotional torment that leave them mentally shattered in the end.

MONEY

Money is vitally important in marriage. It lacks can stir many conflicts, but too much of it could be just as problematic. Who has or controls more money is a delicate topic in many marriages?

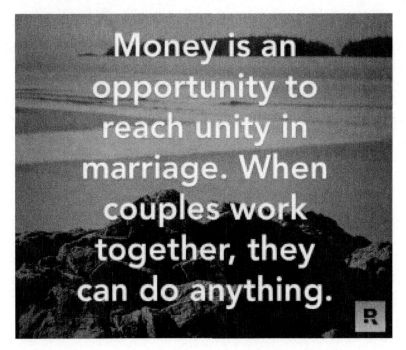

Money is an opportunity to reach unity in marriage. When couples work together, they can do anything.

Ultimately, it's important "each partner must keep in mind that most relationships aren't destroyed by one dramatic act, but a series of small, even individually inconsequential acts that chip away at your foundation of love and trust." - Mary Crary.

Although I got married according to the Islamic injunction my father being Muslim, I had this scripture written on my wedding invitation:

> 1 Corinthians 13:4-5: "Love is patient, love is kind. It does not envy, it does not boast, it is not proud. It does not dishonour others, it is not self-seeking, it is not easily angered, it keeps no record of wrongs."

In the beginning it was a love story, pure and perfect... But somewhere along the way we lost it and it became bitter, full of pain and hurt. The indifferences set in, and each went their own way until we separated amicably.

CHAPTER SEVEN

THE SIMPLE STRATEGY TO BE DELIVERED FROM THE MESS

CHAPTER SEVEN

THE SIMPLE STRATEGY TO BE DELIVERED FROM THE MESS

This was the simple strategy I turned to. Reflecting on my marital journey, I had reasons to not jump ship in the face of mounting challenges. However, staying put was both mentally tough and overwhelming.

I needed energy to remain focused. And I did by using a few simple strategies.

The most important? – God's Word

By now, you are intricately aware of some of my bitter experiences in life. But a quick walk back to 2008. I was going through yet another incredibly challenging time in my role as an Account Officer to one of our clients.

There arose several issues bordering on late delivery of equipment funded by the bank (a dredger) and other issues, so I was placed on suspension.

Initially, I passed it off as a minor issue that would be resolved quickly since I wasn't in the wrong. However, days crept into weeks until it was two months with all of my savings almost dried up. Rent, school fees and bills were mounting. Even putting food on the table was becoming a major challenge. I had no choice but to push aside dignity. So, I reached out to my husband for help, but he simply told me to "fuck off" (we were already separated at this time).

I remember this particular day. I was in a private library in Ikoyi (donated by a philanthropist – Zacchaeus Onumba Dibiaezue Memorial Libraries) preparing for my Certificate in Financial Planning final exam (Institute of Financial Planning, University of Lagos). I went in as soon as the library opened and pored through my books until noon. I kept reading the same page for hours on end. But nothing stuck.

So, I decided to take a break mid-day. Plunged to the back of my car, my heart heavy, barely holding back teary eyes, I told myself that I would not give the devil the twisted satisfaction of seeing me cry. I mustered enough strength to talk to God:

"Dear Lord, I am at this very moment completely exhausted and drained, I have no strength to carry on, and you will have to carry me as I cannot bear anymore. Please Father speak to me".

I picked up my small bible from my bag – no mobile phones or apps back then - and opened it. The scripture that jumped out.

> *Habakkuk 3:19 – "The Lord God is my strength, and he will make my feet like hinds' feet, and he will make me walk upon mine high places".*

"God, the Lord, is my strength;
he makes my feet like the deer's;
he makes me tread on my high places."
Habakkuk 3:19

I read it aloud over and over again. My soul, like a dry sponge, soaked it in until I was completely absorbed. Rejuvenated, I went back into the library elevated and revived.

I looked up the meaning of Hind (a Mountain Goat/ Bighorn Sheep found in the rocky terrains of Israel). They climb high up to uppermost crags, and run over rock fields as easily as we do on beach.

How are Bighorn Sheep able to do this?

Their feet – equipped with tough, cloven hooves. These hooves don't feel hurt on sharp rocks and are strong enough to grip even small outcrops.

Perfectly designed for climbing, they don't slip and do not fall.

The point here is not the *Power* of the sheep, but the <u>design of the sheep's foot.</u>

Habakkuk uses the word for the female deer, not the male, to make this point.

The female deer is able to climb to the highest heights to run over rocky fields because of her special feet.

God assured me that day that he specially designed my feet to climb my high places by HIS STRENGTH.

My life's journey, right from the womb, has been one of trials after trials. And some were self-inflicted, thanks to my easy, carefree personality. Still, I managed to ascend my mountains by <u>HIS STRENGTH</u>.

A dear close friend of mine Pst Tayo Olushola once said to me, "Debbie, since I have known you, it has always been one thing after the other. For The Devil to be coming after you always with a scud missile, then there is something you carry that he doesn't want you to manifest. No one seeing your beautiful, always smiling face will have any inkling of the challenges and troubles you go through". I went home that day comforted.

I continued to prepare for the exams, trusting God for a miracle to pay the fees. By now, I had been informed I won't be allowed to sit the exam if fees were not paid, essentially putting my graduation on the brink of collapse till the following session.

I was running out of time. So I spoke to the program coordinator. I had an idea she would discuss my case with the program director to allow me sit the exam, while I only see my results after completing the fees. But the coordinator refused this arrangement.

It was now Friday, only three days left to the exam day on Monday. I became frantic.

I called a couple of friends to help out with the money but it was a fruitless exercise - some genuinely couldn't help, some deliberately refused to, some promised to call back but never did, some mocked me, some did not even answer my calls and messages or returned them. Others still offered to help, but in exchange for sleeping with them.

My suspension uncovered a lot of lessons. Above all one thing was clear - people prey on the vulnerable. They would not help even if they could unless you parted with your dignity.

That hurts. And doubly so when it came from people I had considered friends. People I trusted.

As it turned out my help came from God, using strangers to meet my needs. By Saturday, my case looked hopeless. I remember sitting on my bedroom floor. Weeping. I ran out of all tears reserves until I started bleeding – a vein broke. When I saw the blood, I stopped crying.

I have heard people mention crying blood. I never knew it was a thing until I did.

> Then I remembered a scripture in **Psalm 121:1** – "*I will lift up my eyes unto the hills, from whence cometh my help?*"

I cried out aloud to Him - the helper of the helpless

I stayed in that position, hopeless for a while until that word of the Lord stuck within me and then I felt peace.

I slept off. Only to wake up to my phone ringing.

It was the coordinator.

She said she had called to tell me to make sure I attend the exam on Monday.

And that she would give me a cheque for the fees, to be repaid anytime I had money. I was overjoyed!

At the exam venue, the program director also came to tell me he had reconsidered my case, and that I would be allowed to write the exam but only get my certificate after paying my fees in full.

The feeling? Just otherworldly. I returned the lady's cheque and appreciated her kindness.

God indeed works miracles.

Dear reader, God is real and His word is forever guaranteed.

Regardless of your situation, however difficult, always remember God has a word for you. Search the scriptures and claim it for God honours His words without fail.

> *Isaiah 55:11 (King James Version) – "So shall my word be that goeth forth out of my mouth, it shall not return unto me void, but it shall accomplish that which I please and it shall prosper in the thing whereto I sent it"*

Brenton Septuagint Translation – "*So shall my word be, whatever shall proceed out of my mouth, it shall by no means turn back, until all the things which I willed shall have been accomplished; and I will make thy ways prosperous and will efftect my commands*"

Good News Translation – "*So also will be the word that I speak – It will not fail to do what I plan for it; it will do everything I send it to do*".

> **Psalm 138:2 (King James Version)** – "*I will worship toward thy holy temple and praise thy name for thy loving kindness and for thy truth; for thou hast magnified thy <u>word above all thy name</u>*".

All glory to God, I passed the exams in flying colours and the institute used the photograph of me receiving my certificate for the course marketing materials for the next session.

The four reasons I stayed in the relationship despite the challenges?

God's Word

Children

Belief

Self

The strategies I turned to, to stay focused while battling the following challenges:

- Financial fix
- No intimacy
- No support

» First, I focused on God's promises because His words never fail.
» Second, I believed in myself, in my capacity to make things work, to make my husband love me.
» I reckoned that after a tiring day working outside, a man should only come back to a homely place for rest.
» So I made my home as comfortable as possible. Cooked meals on time. Always his favourites, prepared for him any time he was around.
» I also had to skill up professionally.
» Anyone familiar with me knows I find learning inseperable from me.
» But more importantly, I implemented what I learned.
» I am someone who believes in continous self-development.
» I would spend any spare time listening to personal development programs on YouTube and self-development books.
» Professionally, I wanted to be a stock broker. But after a while I gave up, I did not pass the exam. Then I left it and also tried to do the ACCA Exam, that

too proved difficult. I just could not cope with those courses. Combining studies, work, children and marital problems put my wellbeing on the edge.

Shortly after the argument on the sexual enhancement drugs, I travelled to Nigeria (2016) and while I was there, my father passed away. It was very traumatic for me. We must realise that we are not meant to be here forever. And just as my dad had to exit, so will every one of us. Now it was time to focus on my career.

I decided to retrain myself and studied for one year to qualify as a mortgage advisor. It was quite difficult both financially and emotionally because by then, he had stopped communicating with me and my two children were now at the university. It was just the two of us at home, a period we continued to spend keeping malice instead of maximising solitude like a new couple.

I had some wonderful friends, people who were both my mentors and cheerleaders. They kept encouraging me - Debbie, you can do it just keep on.

I remember going for the final exam, done at a computer-based centre. After hitting the submit button, the computer processes and turns in your score in five minutes or less. I failed the exam narrowly, falling short of two marks. So, I registered to retake the exam immediately and took the exam a week after.

Again, I failed, by five marks or so.

I became upset, but also more determined to succeed. One of my mentors Mr. Olushola Makinwa advised me to look up further resources online. I did and came across a company that provided 10 years' worth of exam questions I gladly purchased. Practice after practice, I became more confident. I struck off my failed score on the last exam result and wrote 95%, tricking my subconscious into scoring that high in my next trial. The time came to resit the exam. It was the last day of the academic session (31st August) ... And this time?

Well, I finished ahead of time but couldn't hit the submit button. My past trials still flashing through my mind.

I eventually mustered courage, shut my eyes and allowed the computer to process my grade. Counting to fifty, I opened my eyes.

And. saw...

CONGRATULATIONS YOU PASSED!!!!!

> *"Even if you are the only one who believes in your dream if you are committed to it, you will achieve it."*
>
> *Kate Iroegbu*

It felt surreal. I had just won my monster. Too weak and wobbly, I dragged my legs to the ladies' room (toilet) for relief, thanking God as I struggled to stave off teary eyes. Outside was Tony, my mentor who had been waiting by the car all along. I was visibly shaking, so he asked how things panned out.

When I tried to speak, my eyes couldn't hold back any longer. I just burst out in tears wailing. He started to comfort me and then I passed the results notification to him. Seeing I had passed, he was very happy for me. "So why are you crying silly child?" he asked. Just tears of joy. After all the grinding I had done, I finally achieved victory. I created a better version of myself. My core values are focused on one of God's promises from the Bible verse Habakkuk 3:19.

Children

I lost my mother when I was just a little over a year old. I still miss the vacuum of never knowing her. I did not want my children to grow up without one and suffering the same way I did. Hence, my children were my driving force.

Every time I think about them, and I say to myself

"I'm alive and things are like this for them." So, if I allowed myself to lose focus or drop dead, my children were going to suffer and I don't want them to go through that suffering, so it kept me going

Determined that my children will never go hungry, I focused on my work, gave it my best shot, and was regularly promoted.

Belief

Being raised a Christian, the Bible states clearly that God hates divorce.

The church does not support divorce, so I kept my faith.

I kept praying and trusting God to make away. For God to change him and his unbelief.

There's nothing that God cannot do, but there are also certain things that God will not do. The one mistake ladies make is to marry a person thinking that they can change that person.

The Bible makes us understand that we can only change with the help of The Holy Spirit, who can convict us of sin, righteousness, and judgement? You cannot change any person. The only person you can change is yourself.

So, after years of battle, self-doubts, bitterness, anger and the rest of the work.

Like Leah, I learned to now focus on God and myself, I focused on changing myself.

Self

I wanted my marriage to succeed you know. For obvious reasons.

As an African (and specifically Nigerian) woman, divorce meant ridicule:

"Oh, how many husbands has she had? How many men does she have children with?" I didn't want to leave that sort of legacy behind for me or my children.

So, I wanted things to work at all costs. I was driven to succeed in my career and marital life. And there were challenges along the way.

But I made decisions and took actions that, in hindsight, the wiser me wouldn't have taken. But at the time and circumstances, I did what I felt was best.

My driving force was only God, my children and my life. I was determined to remain alive, and I will always be determined to remain alive. Often, I would say to myself. You see, my mother died at 32, I am not going to die, not one nanosecond earlier than God has ordained for me, in Jesus' name, Amen.

I know that God's plans for me are for good and not for evil.

I was created for a purpose and that purpose must be fulfilled because at the end of my days, I want to stand before my creator and hear him say "Well done my good and faithful servant, enter into your rest.".

Not one word from God will fail without being fulfilled.

No matter what you are passing through, hold on tight to God.

Never Let go of God.

CHAPTER EIGHT

AN INDUSTRIOUS WOMAN IN AN AFRICAN CLIME

CHAPTER EIGHT

AN INDUSTRIOUS WOMAN IN AN AFRICAN CLIME

The African tradition holds men as leaders, the head of the home who should in turn be treated with utmost respect and honour. These values were further ingrained in me growing up as a Yoruba woman. To be subservient to your husband, obey his wishes, cook, clean, raise the kids and support both immediate and extended family members.

I held the belief that my role as a wife was to support my husband, to build together a life where we can both grow and achieve things together. A wife is supposed to be a helpmate to her husband.

Marriage is more than just having children or satisfying primal desires. Anyone can have children without necessarily getting married. But God instituted marriage for a purpose. Why? Because Adam was lonely in the garden of Eden and it wasn't good, So God gave him Eve. A partner to keep him company and to assist him to fulfil his mission and succeed in life. God made the woman special. The presence of a good woman in a man's life leads to expansion, increase and enlargement.

The woman has both a physical womb (designed to nurture her husband's seeds and raise babies to continue worldly existence) and a spiritual womb that stores her God-given gifts and treasures to complement the man and fulfil the purpose of God on earth. That was what the devil saw, and he became mad and went after the woman vigorously and she fell but God never gave up on her and made a way of escape.

According to Dr Myles Munroe, whatever you give to a woman she multiplies. The most terrible thing that can happen to any lady is to marry a man without vision, so it's best for you to wait for the right man (the perfect will of God for your life), a man who knows his purpose, and with whom you can partner to fulfil destiny.

I believed I was my husband's helpmate and took the responsibilities as such. Apart from being educated, I also had entrepreneurial skills and was blessed with a high paying professional job, so paying the bills wasn't a problem. I earned far more and was just being support-ive, I thought.

But my naivety brought more problems than it solved. I found it strange and unexplainable, difficult to wrap my head around. A working, helpful supportive wife, I thought I was the perfect woman, a man's dream. But a station of high esteem turned into my avenue for problems.

Accommodation Issues

During my one-year NYSC in Lagos, my father made arranged that I stayed with my uncle. It was a room in a house which I shared with my two children, my husband's cousin and sometimes my husband when he came around, making us five. I lived in that room for almost two years. We continued to stay there after my service year till I got a better paying job.

Then it happened that a flat in one of my father's properties became vacant. So, he told me to think about it with my husband. I discussed the idea of moving there with him and, while initially reluctant, he eventually agreed.

But there was one condition, I reasoned. I told my dad we would only take it on the condition that we would pay the rent. I come from a polygamous family and wouldn't tolerate anyone disrespecting my husband. I never got wind my husband's "yes" actually meant "no". I mean; how does a man say yes and expect his wife to believe he said no? (Well, men generally think a woman means yes when she is saying no). And that breeds confusion. So let your words mean what you say- Yes or No.

I only wanted some comfort for us, but he reasoned otherwise and communicated it in no way I understood. So, I went ahead, refurbished the flat to taste and made it as comfortable as possible. He wasn't happy with this, did not mention anything about it at the time but kept the grudge against me. This was another crack in the marriage. I believed I was helping, sincerely. Even a billionaire married man still needs this value-add of his woman (and value doesn't necessarily mean money).

In hindsight, I believe he felt threatened by my success. He wouldn't, when asked, hesitate to say I treated him arrogantly.

Perhaps he felt unsettled seeing the student he once taught become both a financially independent and supporting wife.

Our Car Rift

This incident I knew hurt him deeply. I took my car back from him. We agreed to buy a car from the proceeds of a job bonus. Then I drove to Ijebu ode for the annual Ileya festival. He had informed his family of our new car. But I was taken aback when, after the holidays, I discovered he expected me to leave the car for him. Despite the fact, that I lived in Lagos with the children, while he stays at Ijebu Ode. Well, for peace to reign, I let him have his way and he took us back to Lagos.

The arrangement was that he would visit us more often at weekends. But he wasn't keeping to the agreement

It was on a morning. I was getting ready for work and hurrying to catch the staff bus at 5:45 am.

And it was raining that morning and he was getting ready to drive back to his place in Ago-Iwoye. He didn't feel obliged to at least take me to the bus stop, and so I had to walk the 12-minute distance drenched in rain.

It was then I decided I would take my car back when next he visits. Of course, a litany of disagreements followed, and my father had to step in. He demanded that I returned the car to him, which I did. Only to take my keys back when we got back home. I told him to buy his car if he needed one.

You see, anger, if not properly managed, can be a destroyer. And that incident, it turned out, was my greatest sin, one he ultimately couldn't forgive and move on from.

A Supportive Woman and a Loving Husband

The Bible says that one will chase a thousand and two shall chase 10,000. Unity in a marriage is very, very, very important. United couples go farther together, and it's not hard to see why. I'll share a story.

At about the same time we did, another couple moved to the UK. But they are Christian, a true believer in the gospel of the Lord. Any issues they had; they would flesh out together. They would usually give testimonies in church, how they sat down, wrote down their plans for their family for the year and together they will pray about it, and then tackle ensuing challenges head-on. Sometimes, even before mid-year, they would give testimonies that all their prayer requests for the year had already been answered. I share this example to let you in on how important husband-wife unity is for marital progress.

Another couple very dear to my heart, I've known this family for more than 20 years. On their wedding day, something unexpected happened and they had no place to spend their honeymoon on their first night.

They had to shelter in a friend's house. And things stayed rough in their early years. Today? They are both comfortable and very successful. Was it fun? No. Did they have an easy ride? No. But what they did have - their faith in God, their love and trust for each other. And that was all they needed to overcome their challenges to success.

Again, the point I'm making, and I would like you to pay attention to is that marriage doesn't work if couples don't do the work.

A successful marriage requires unity, with that union with God as the head. It takes a lot of commitment. It takes a lot of forgiveness. It takes a lot of prayers. It takes a lot of agreement. It takes a lot of love between the two - for marriage to work.

The Jobs and The Businesses I Had

I engaged in buying and selling small items to keep myself busy while waiting for NYSC posting, using the One Thousand Naira bursary award received from university. This was a homebased business of selling iced water and soft drinks. The business grew from four crates to fifty-two crates over eight months.

Since my post-Youth Service days, I worked in the finance industry - in the banking sector for about 12 years. I left and then went to become self-employed, leveraging the skills I acquired over the years in sales, marketing, and customer service adviser to start my own business.

Also, I opened a supermarket, which included clothing and garments for children and ladies. Whenever I came to the UK on holidays, I would restock by buying children's clothing and ladies' outfits to sell in my store. Profit from these businesses were used to support for my family.

I registered a company delivering diesel to companies. Grew so successful I secured a contract to deliver trailers of diesel to Nigerian Port Authority vessels before leaving Nigeria. So, it was a tough call for me to decide to move to the UK, leaving behind my successes to build again from scratch. But I took the step of faith and believed in my decision to move to England.

Once, in my room, I had one of my many conversations with God. Truly, I was reluctant to move because my business was doing well. My relationship with my husband wasn't great, we had separated for over two years, but we settled shortly before he came to the UK - three and a half years before my children and I joined him.

Then reports I heard about life in the UK complicated things more.

Black children and boys getting targeted or killed, especially in London? Relocating didn't particularly sound good. I was scared and fearful of regret in later years. What if I sent my children to the UK while I stayed back in Nigeria, focusing on business?

So, this day, I was in my room just talking with God. And I said to the Lord, if He truly wanted me to go to the UK, please show me (like Gideon in the bible, I put the fleece out before God) I said this man, my husband that's looking for accommodation because he lived in the Southeast London. And he didn't want to raise our children in that neighbourhood, so he was looking for accommodation in the East of London.

So, I said, Lord, prove to me that you want me to relocate to London, let my husband find accommodation in a place where there's a Redeemed Christian Church of God that is a walking distance from the property he will rent. I said that prayer or that conversation with God and I left it and a few days later we travelled to the UK.

We arrived in London on the 31st of August. And then

on the first of September, we both went to East London and collected the keys to the apartment he had rented from the estate agent and were to look at the property. As we were going, we walked on the left side of the road path and crossed over to the apartment. We inspected everything collected the keys and then we're returning home walking towards the station and lo and behold, guess what I saw? A Redeemed Christian Church of God signboard. I was so shocked. I stopped suddenly and he was surprised wondering what was happening. What! What? I said See! See! See! Pointing to the church. Yeah, of course, he was like and so what the heck? Well, he didn't know about the conversation I had with God. I got really interested in the things of God of which I was a member of The Redeemed Christian Church of God. When I was in Nigeria.

Its mission is to have a church. Five minutes' drive for anyone in urban areas, and five minutes' walk in rural areas. God proved to me that he wanted me to come to the United Kingdom and he heard my prayer. The distance from the apartment my husband got to where the church was, was like a four minutes' walk. Yeah, you had me right. Four minutes' walk. So, in the years I've been in this country when things got tough and I start to moan God, why did I come to this country? I want to go back to Nigeria; I want to go back home. I would remember my conversation with God and the way He answered, and I would be comforted.

*God actually can be comical sometimes you know, a four-minute strolling distance, not even brisk walking, when the standard requirement was 5 mins walking distanc*e. So, that was my conviction that yes, God wanted me to come here. So, no matter what I faced, I sucked it up. And I just kept on.

I encourage everyone to also read **Kate Iroegbu's book – Triumph in the Midst of Adversity.** Tough times never last, only tough people do. Everyone faces life challenges, but what counts the most is what you do while at it. **Reflecting on Kelly Clarkson, song--- what doesn't kill you makes you stronger.**

Drawing on My Experience

I was raised by parents who epitomised unity. Everything they did, they did together. And I regard that as the most sure-fire way to marital success. My education and well-paid job meant I could help pay bills and raise our kids the best way I knew. But I came across as arrogant, or so my husband considered me.

A quick word to readers – single or married. If you are with a hardworking/supportive woman, contempt and taking them for granted are ways you never want to treat them. Bliss blossoms when you treat your spouse as invaluable, when you cherish them, appreciate them.

Cliché but true - Behind every successful man is a supportive woman.

So, make harmony non-negotiable, because your success depends on it. I mean, just imagine a depressed pilot with a shattered home flying a commercial plane. The end result is anyone's guess.

CHAPTER NINE

MY SUCCESS WAS A THREAT.

CHAPTER NINE

MY SUCCESS WAS A THREAT

How?

In many ways, as I look back in hindsight.

At work, by the grace of God and by my diligence, I often got promoted swiftly and had perks like upfront allowances, salary increases, bonuses, and performance-based profit sharing at the end of the financial year. Add this all up and you have a decent sum of money to pour into capital investment. But every time I received such payments, I would gleefully show him the letter.

Once, I got paid and asked him in what we should invest? A gym, he said. But I reasoned that would not be viable. You see, university students struggle to feed and get course materials. as they are not obliged to receive student funding as in some other nations in the world. So, paying a regular gym subscription wouldn't really be a thing for them.

Further, there were unpredictable university strikes,

during which university will be closed, forcing students to go home for months.

My suggestion to him? Let's buy half a plot of land and build maybe six studio flats on it, then rent them out to students (the university ran off-campus accommodation and getting a decent place was always an issue). If we went for this, we would always get annual rental income, whether ASUU went on strike or not. But he did not buy my idea. So, we moved on. There were other times we differed on investment choices, perhaps we saw things differently.

What would I have done differently?

In hindsight, I probably should have allowed him to take the decision he thought best. As an African man and head of the family, he probably felt undermined accepting my opposing ideas on how best to spend my money.

Maybe the change in my lifestyle?

He also argued I was living large - cars, clothes, accommodation, travel abroad for holidays, whatever I really wanted I could afford without waiting for his money. That probably sent arrogant vibes to him.

What did I learn from this?

I should probably have been more patient. I mean, let

him have his way sometimes even if I felt it wasn't the right thing to do. Better problem-solving and negotiation skills would have helped.

So, looking back, I would take decisions by writing down the pros and cons of our choices on a sheet of paper and our agreement would have been amicable either way. This would make him feel that I was deliberating with him, not doing things at my bidding.

It would have removed ego from the way so I wouldn't appear as sole financier of the project. One strategy would have been to come up to him with a plan, where I go "okay, let's set up a joint venture with both of us investing this amount of money," so he has funds committed and we both share any gain or loss.

Sure, staying fit and healthy meant a gym wasn't a bad idea. But students were our target market, and they dominated the area, so the environment did not align. Hairdressers, food restaurants, transport etc., other businesses in this area also suffered a dip whenever students were not around.

If he had brought his business idea and we set up as partners, we would have come up with ways to maximize profit potential while reducing the knock-on effects of ASUU strike and other influences outside our control.

This approach would probably have worked. But my simple basic risk analysis drove my suggestion and I was only deeply focused on profitable multiple streams of income, so we were not entirely dependent on our salaries.

While I only tried to better our collective lot and expand our income sources, he saw my efforts as arrogance.

The additional income would have steadied our household income, in turn easing the financial burden on me since I took care of nearly all the bills.

Choice of School

Choosing a private school for my children was also an issue. There were times I had issues at work and needed financial help to pay my children's school fees. He had none of that, saying I made the choice to live large and should enrol them in a cheaper school if I couldn't manage.

I married someone I thought would support me down the line to give our kids the best quality education, but he wouldn't see the necessity of that. Then, I took it upon myself as a major investment on my children, similar to the story of our ICON, singer, actress, and song writer - Onyeka Onwenu, who funded her two sons' education to a master's degree solely by herself as a married woman. Bizarre how some of us live the widow life while married. But my investment paid off as I saw my children grow in admirable ways. I could compromise all else, but not a solid educational foundation.

I realise he was more content if I was a totally dependent wife. A woman who was entirely reliant on her husband for everything finance. Sometimes you don't really know what a man needs.

I mean, are you really out for a liability as a wife? Or a hardworking companion and helpmeet?

Initially, I was economically dependent on him for everything, and peace reigned. But things changed once I steadily began to earn my own money. To men reading this book, know that complete financial control of your immediate family is something good, but if things are difficult despite going above and beyond, a financially buoyant and helpful wife is a blessing that removes no bit from your worth.

Women can assist their spouses in more ways than one. Today, many women abound with vast potential to birth and live a life both pleasing to you and your creator. But in the face of evident need, stumbling on their path could impede both her potential and that of the family. Realise that God has endowed many women with such attributes and blessings that do not conflict with your worth as a man and the healthy living of the family. I humbly consider myself one such woman.

And I believe in an atmosphere of love, respect, and humility, living with such women only breeds a blissful marital life.

I was favoured with financially rewording jobs throughout my career and would have benefitted more in the company of a supporting husband who helped me channel these blessings to the right places, instead of abandoning me to work the responsibilities of two in stressful conditions that stretched my sanity to the limit.

DEBBIE OLABISI

CHAPTER TEN

THE WAY FORWARD

CHAPTER TEN

THE WAY FORWARD

As you already know. Life's difficulties are a time of opportunities. Tough times can be a pain, but after every pain is ease, and after every darkness is light. If you manage to look beyond the pain, you will not only see light at the end of the tunnel but become a distributor of light.

After reflecting and asking myself some deep questions, I realise that indeed I am a warrior - in the battlefield of life. And I have been honoured through God's faithfulness through it all.

Perhaps you are in a similar situation or experiencing lows in your marital life. I have one message for you – don't give up. Keep at it. Try working out issues with your spouse. But if all else fails, do not be hard on yourself. Remember, marriage works when two people agree to put in the work. If you have prayed consistently, exhausted all ideas but your spouse still would not resolve differences, accept things in good faith. Do not die in it, as I almost did, enduring a torturous 24 years of marital distress before calling it a day.

I often ask myself some questions, deliberate key questions as I tried to gain clarity of my situation.

Was I single? -No, I had a husband.

Was I truly married? – No, I never truly enjoyed any marital benefits.

Was I separated? - Probably, because we lived more separately than together in our 24 years of marriage.

Was I a widow? – Definitely, not. Because my husband is alive but stayed aloof from my life and our children.

So, if I was married, what sort of marriage would this be called?

If I were to choose staying single or living this type of marital life, what option would I go for?

So, what adjective would I be qualified with in my situation?

Since I hated divorce but also knew I wasn't married in the real sense of the word, staying put almost ruined my existence to death. If I had sought medical intervention, I mostly likely would have been placed on a heavy dose of anti-depressants.

It got to a time when I had to decide.

Stay and DIE or Leave TO LIVE?

I chose the second option - leave to live. And I believe this to be one of the best life decisions I ever made. Otherwise, no one would be sharing this story in a book titled - Married for 24 Years but Living Single.

But I am here putting my story down in black and white with the help of Kate Iroegbu of TriumphInThe-MidstofAdversity.com Ltd and looking forward to the launch of my book on my 50th birthday celebration here in London, United Kingdom on the 14th of May 2022. I am super excited.

If I had chosen the first option - to STAY and DIE, I probably would have been a forgotten story related to my children from anyone who cared to listen at all

In the end, we've all got ONLY ONE LIFE TO LIVE.

And, when old, I prefer sitting grey-haired in my rocking chair, enjoying the cool breeze of the day smiling and recounting a life of accomplishments and happy memories with no room for regrets... Life is too short.

I was born for a purpose, and I must fulfil that purpose as God does not waste His resources.

Are you presently there? Married, either by tradition, religion or by law and you are in pain, agony or fear? Are you asking yourself what is going on here?

I *get* you. And how your feel.

I understand your deep pains of ill treatment, of scorn, of a loveless marriage. But always remember, only the two partners in a sinking marriage can rescue it. So, fight for the ship you built, but don't sink with it if all else fails.

Being married for 24 years but living single was no child's play. It took the grace of God, love for my children, my core values, circle of support and believing that it is not over with me – to wade through the hurt.

Les Brown said "It is Not Over Until I win"

My marriage may not have worked out, and despite trying hard and doing everything humanly possible, I was faced with rejection, abuse, and enmity, but the woman in me only wanted a husband - a best friend, a darling, a lover, someone to look after me physically and emotionally. I wanted a man to protect and lead me, to respect me even when our beliefs differed, someone sensitive to my needs, thoughts, and feelings. A spouse accepting of my faults, supportive of my endeavours, interested in my job, welcoming of my problems, passionate, trustworthy, and someone who turned to effective communication, committing to talk things through no matter how difficult. Someone to grow old with.

Dear reader/friend do not feel disappointed. Do not give up on yourself. Read and learn from some of my life lessons. Sometimes you get it right from the beginning.

Not so other times.

> *A successful marriage is a journey of two committed forgivers.*

But not for my choice, who knows? I may have been a forgotten entity in the vastness of time, my story only to be mentioned by anyone who knew me to anyone who cared to listen. But I hope my first-hand account brought you a healthy dose of lessons.

Make no mistake, marriage is sweet. But only if you factor God in your choice of partner, and if you both are committed to making it work. Forgiveness is your marital lifeblood, without which your odds of success are little to none. This is key because two people from different backgrounds and upbringings would naturally meet a sour melting point in the absence of commitment and forgiveness.

The Bible says can one lie alone and be warm? The Bible also says one will chase one thousand and two will chase ten thousand.

A marriage of two committed, like-minded individuals is a time-tested recipe for success. Together, you will blossom to achieve shared goals. And, when old and grey, continue to be friends, loving each other's company till death.

In conclusion: Amos 3:3 Can two walk together, except they agree?

BE NOT UNEQUALLY YOKED

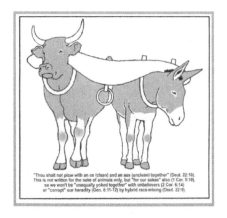

"Thou shalt not plow with an ox (clean) and an ass (unclean) together" (Deut. 22:10).
This is not written for the sake of animals only, but "for our sakes" also (1 Cor. 9:10),
so we won't be "unequally yoked together" with unbelievers (2 Cor. 6:14)
or "corrupt" our heredity (Gen. 6:11-12) by hybrid race-mixing (Deut. 22:9).

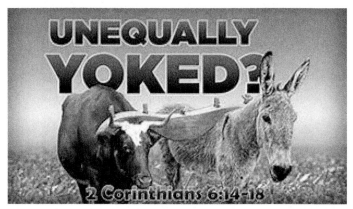

In every area of your life be very mindful of your close associations, because they will impact your life. In a big way.

WHAT WOULD YOU LIKE TO BE INSCRIBED ON YOUR HEAD STONE WHEN YOU DIE?

YOU BEAT LIFE BY STANDING UP AGAIN!!!! EVEN IF YOU FALL 10X

STAND UP AGAIN!!!!!

WHAT I AM DOING PRESENTLY

Best Selling Author, A Speaker, Mortgage Adviser and Specialist Protection Adviser.

Photo of Debbie speaking at ICAN conference in London, United Kingdom, March 2022.

Featured in Who's A Celebrity Magazine, Jan/April 2022, kindly get a copy and read my recent article on Wills, Lasting Powers of Attorney, Trust, and Pre-paid funeral plans. This is vital and must not shy away from it.

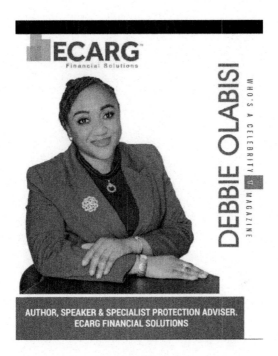

ECARG
Financial Solutions

DEBBIE OLABISI

WHO'S A CELEBRITY MAGAZINE

AUTHOR, SPEAKER & SPECIALIST PROTECTION ADVISER.
ECARG FINANCIAL SOLUTIONS

SPECIALISING IN

- Wills
- Lasting Powers of Attorney
- Trusts
- Pre-paid Funeral Plans

IT IS PARTICULARLY IMPORTANT FOR YOU TO CONSIDER PUTTING THESE IN PLACE IF YOU:

Are a single parent, married/divorced or planning to get married.

Are a cohabiting couple who are not married or in a civil partnership.

Have children from a previous relationship.

Have dependents or a business.

Are retired and need to update an existing one.

What is a Will and why should you write one?

A Will is an important legal document in which the Will maker (also known as a testator) can state how they would like their belongings (assets, chattels and property) to be distributed when they are no longer around. The document also gives special people (called executors) the power to handle the estate after the Will Maker's death.

Are you looking at will writing, insurance, mortgage and estate planning?

Get in touch

enquiries@ecargfinancialsolutions.co.uk

SUMMARY

Zig Ziglar said- You are where you are because that's exactly where you chose to be....

Life is all about making choices, and with each choice comes its rewards or consequences.

The ONLY choice we cannot make is who our birth parents are.

As a child, I came to the realisation that I was different. What made me so I couldn't tell and there was no one to tell me. Thus began my journey of finding me, finding love, acceptance, stability and a safe cocoon. Each step of the journey was wrought with challenges, so unusual that I began to think perhaps I was supposed to have been born male but due to something happening I came out female. From childhood through teens and adulthood I forged through conquest after conquest. Many at times I fell, wounded and bleeding, nearly dying, but always He sends help to raise up this wounded soldier. I found love and a safe haven to rest and build my nest, but alas, that was short lived and then began the journey of rejection. In the bid to restore that which was lost, I began to ask questions, what happened here? How did we get here, so far off our expected destination?

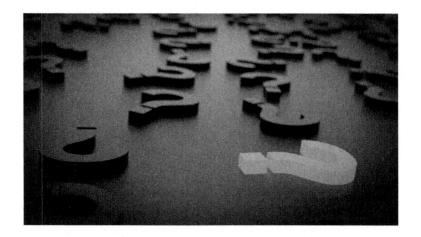

How do we repair the damage? Is there still any way to revive the love that is now dead? Where is the way forward?

Then the final choice had to be made - Stay and continue dying? Or leave and take a chance to Live....

I chose life, and an abundant one.

Never give up on yourself, make the choice to live and make the most of it because you have got ONLY ONE LIFE!!!!!

Thank you for reading.

And I hope this book helps you in your marital journey and life lessons.

Kindly leave a review on Amazon.

Do not forget to follow me on my social media handles to connect and for updates on my future projects.

See below

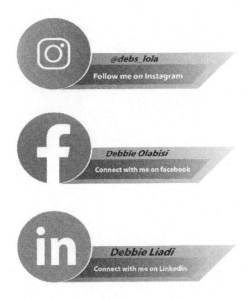

@debs_lola
Follow me on Instagram

Debbie Olabisi
Connect with me on facebook

Debbie Liadi
Connect with me on Linkedin

Printed in Great Britain
by Amazon

80236691R00093